Your Neighbor Went to War

Reality and the War on Terror

Captain B. Diggs Brown, Jr.

United States Army Special Forces

Cover Design by George Foster

Edited by
Denise Hmieleski
P.O. Box 709
Lafayette, CO 80026-0709

Published by Clifton House, U.S.A.
903 Rule Drive, Suite 6
Fort Collins, CO 80525

Visit www.diggs.us

● ● ●

Your Neighbor Went to War – Reality and the War on Terror
B. Diggs Brown, Jr.
ISBN
0-9754158-0-8

Printed in the United States of America
Library of Congress Control Number 2004092360

Contents

Acknowledgments   i

Dedication   iii

Preface   v

1   PREPARING FOR WAR   1

2   OCONUS (Outside Continental United States)   9

3   CORRESPONDING WITH THE CHILDREN   23

4   HOME SWEET HOME   31

5   WINNING THE HEARTS AND MINDS   37

6   TURNING 46 IN AFGHANISTAN   57

7   GROUNDHOG DAY   65

8   CIVILIZATION AT LAST!   71

9   THANKSGIVING / WHERE'S THE HEAT?   77

10   THE CHEERFUL MAN   83

11   TRAGIC TIMES   91

12   MERRY CHRISTMAS WITH THE USO   101

13   MOVING TO BAGRAM   107

14   VERY BAD PEOPLE OUT THERE   113

15   NEW YEAR'S IN THE "BIG A"   117

16   AFGHAN OVERFLIGHT   121

17   THE THINGS WE TAKE FOR GRANTED   129

18   HOMESICK   135

19 BURNS NIGHT SUPPER WITH THE SCOTS   139

20 MORE LETTERS FROM THE CHILDREN   143

21 AN AMERICAN IN PARIS   149

22 REBIRTH OF A NATION   153

23 WRAPPING THINGS UP   163

24 HOMEWARD BOUND   171

25 HOME AT LAST!   179

26 LAST THOUGHTS   193

Photo Credits   197

About the Author   199

Glossary   201

Afghanistan Quick Facts   203

ACKNOWLEDGMENTS

Life is of little consequence unless you can share your experiences and help others reach their potential. I never expected my letters home to have the influence that they did on both sides of the ocean. Likewise, the letters that were sent to me from friends (and sometimes from complete strangers) made me more aware of the compassion and generosity Americans have to offer the world.

In numerous letters, calls, and face-to-face encounters I was asked and advised to write about my experiences during the global war on terrorism in Afghanistan. I really didn't give this much thought until a recent sermon at the church I attend. As I listened to the sermon, which dealt with charity and sharing, I found myself drifting back to the days in Afghanistan when the boxes of school supplies sent from home were distributed to the students at a bombed-out village, Pol-e-charkhi. Emotionally charged after the sermon, I decided the story had to be told.

Another factor contributing to this publication is the ongoing negativity the media has been painting on our efforts in Afghanistan and, most recently, in Iraq. It is time Americans heard the truth of what their military is doing for these desolate people. The Special Forces motto is "Liberate the oppressed," and that is exactly what we did and are continuing to do. Americans no longer have to be the whipping boy of the liberal media. We are good and generous people, often admired and, in some cases, envied by the world. We should have no guilt in the fact that we are a superpower. It is our freedom that enables us to hold that power and to be a symbol of honor and generosity for all humanity.

It is my decision to keep the reader as close to the situation as I can, and this is only possible by using the communiqués both coming and going. This is the best way to share the sense of real time and the interaction on both sides of the ocean. More importantly, there is minimal editing of spelling and grammar, and no editing of the thoughts that were shared. These are the writings of real people opening their hearts and expressing their concerns and innermost convictions. No one can improve upon that.

With that said, I would like to thank all who have written to me and also those who contributed to this effort. And special heartfelt thanks go to all the children who have sent letters addressed "To Any Soldier," no matter which war or generation.

DEDICATION

This dedication is directed to many people: my family and friends for their support, letters, and prayers while I was overseas; the congregation of my church for their prayers; and the countless number of U.S. citizens who wrote letters of encouragement and sent boxes of comfort items to the front lines.

I would also like to dedicate this book to a number of young people, many of the names I will never know. They are the children in Afghanistan who have been given a new chance at life and the children of the United States who unselfishly gave donations of school supplies and hope.

Finally, this book is dedicated to the United States military and those who support them. We are a force of liberation, not occupation, with a compassion for those we free from tyranny. Over 200 years of honing the fine edge of this sword has prepared us for any enemy—as witnessed in the past, experienced in the present, and anticipated for in the future.

God bless all of you.

حق آزادی برای مظلومان

(Liberate the oppressed)

PREFACE

On the morning of September 11, 2001, I was on the verge of being late for a conference call at the bank where I worked. As I hurried out of my condominium, I crossed paths with one of my neighbors. He mentioned that a plane had hit the World Trade Tower, but he failed to say anything about it being a passenger plane. Not having much time to talk, I responded briefly that a plane once hit the Empire State Building in the '40s, so this current incident, while tragic, probably wasn't anything of consequence. I assumed the aircraft was something along the size of a small Cessna.

I arrived at the bank in time to catch the beginning of the conference call. Within seconds of taking my seat, a distraught teller entered the room and told of the second plane striking the towers. At this point, the bank president left the room. Melissa, a fellow employee, and I stayed to continue with the call. My thoughts were elsewhere. I wondered how on earth the conference call could continue.

Minutes later the bank president returned, clearly in distress. The rumor was that as many as 600,000 may have died in the attack. Upon hearing this, I took the initiative and disconnected us from the call. We each went our separate ways to digest the news. Melissa hurried across the street to see her baby at the daycare center. I joined the rest of the employees near a radio to hear the latest. Customers continued to enter the bank, unaware of the world-altering events of the morning.

That evening I stared at the Hollywood-like footage of the attack and eventual collapse of the towers. Like most of the public, I had a difficult time digesting the events of that day. There was utter chaos, which I believe President Bush handled as a true leader would. The uncertainty of my future now held a certainty— I would be going to war. At some point my National Guard unit would be activated, and we would do our duty. With this in mind, I began the assiduous task of getting my life in order.

For the next few months I continued to work at the bank in my position of regional investment manager, overseeing the investment operations for seven banks scattered across northeastern Colorado. I felt obligated to take care of the client base I had established in the three years of commuting to the "far reaches," so I kept working and waiting for word of when my unit would deploy.

In July 2002, my unit was given the warning order for deployment, and we began preparations. Three weeks of training at Fort Polk got our heads into the game and helped us fine-tune our skills. At this point, I left the bank and placed all of my belongings in storage. I wanted to spend my last remaining days as a civilian with family and friends.

With an August report date for active duty, I managed to squeeze in as much time as possible with my family. I even made a trip down to Dallas (where I had lived for 13 years) to see my many friends there. Then, all too soon, it was time to head back to Colorado and then on to active duty.

My association with the children who were writing the letters "To Any Soldier" came as we were boarding the C-5 Galaxy cargo plane that would take us on the first leg of our journey to war. Chaplain Andy (you will read more about him in pages to come) sat beside me on this initial flight, and he had a pile of letters from the children at a Colorado grade school. I was able to sort through these letters and find two children whose letters intrigued me. I remembered when I was in grade school and had sent letters of encouragement to soldiers in Vietnam. I never received a letter of reply from those soldiers, so I vowed to respond to these children.

What you are going to see on the following pages is a compilation of e-mail and "snail mail" to and from family, friends, and the children who, through their own accord, decided to reach out and help the children of Afghanistan. Due to the very real threat to families of Special Forces soldiers by al Qaeda, I have only used the first names of those soldiers involved in this mission.

When you're wounded and left

On Afghanistan's plains,

And the women come out

To cut up your remains,

Jest roll on your rifle,

And blow out your brains,

An' go to your Gawd like a soldier.

— Rudyard Kipling
(*The Young British Soldier*)

CHAPTER 1
PREPARING FOR WAR

Dearest Diggsy:

Well, see...I honestly meant to reach you while you were at your parents', and time has slipped away from me again.

I'm sure you don't have quite the same sense of surrealism about going over, as it is what you've been training for so long. The situation over there has been very real, but not so much as now, with your having to go over. Nothing pisses me off MORE than something that takes away any of the few eligible bachelors still out there!

I'll be thinking of you and praying for you, for your family. I talked to your dad for a while today, and he sounded great and really proud of you and your preparedness for this mission. I have no doubt about that and am proud of you, too.

Take care of yourself, honey. We'll all look forward to word from you whenever you can squeeze it in. Stay away from the women. They maybe don't shave their armpits, either. (ha!)

Much love from Di-O in Ohio...

Diggs,

I'm numbed by this cowardly action on soil, way of life, and our freedom. THEY have waken a sleeping giant and when He gets the WTC dust wiped from his eyes and focuses on the enemy, THEY will understand that they have underestimated our resolve. I figured you'd be out the door by now, so I'll keep this short.

Thought I'd give you some of Gene's Pearls of Combat Wisdom:

1. Keep your powder dry.

2. Smell the wind, remember they stink.

3. One head shot is better than three in the chest.

4. Remember to attack when they blink.

5. *In a war there are no coffee breaks.*

6. *If they run, don't chase. Shoot them in the ass, because the ass you'll save is your own. Know the rules of the game— give no quarter, receive no quarter. There are no rules.*

7. *Don't hate your enemy—hate is an emotion. Do your job.*

8. *Don't bellyache on training, because there is an enemy commander training his troops twice as hard to kill you.*

9. *The enemy will be where you least expect him. Look at the least expected.*

10. *Stay out of the trees and nut busting rocks. Fight your war, not his.*

> *Stay low,*
> *Gene*

Dear Diggs,

I just want you to know that I do not take your leaving lightly. When I said good-bye at the last dinner/seminar I knew I had to make it a quick hug and a kiss because I surely would have started to blubber...and then, being the sensitive-type guy that you are, you might have gotten all emotional, too. I wouldn't have minded that if we hadn't been around your associates and customers.

Anyway, dear friend, now that I have a Higher Power at this time in my life, I will be using it to ask that your time fighting for our country moves swiftly, that you are always safe, and that you know you're in my thoughts and prayers. And when you're back here telling war stories, the margs will be on me!

God Bless America, and God Bless You!

> *Love and XO,*
> *Kath*

Diggs,

I must say that our conversation on Saturday has been weighing heavy on my heart. You see, I woke up at 8:57 AM (I had the alarm set) and then the phone rang at 9:00 AM (I looked at the clock when the phone rang). It was great to hear from you. I hoped that you were calling to say that we would be taking a road trip together soon and so I was completely caught off guard by the topic of conversation.

Diggs Brown is my Hero and when he called me on Saturday to ask me what he should put me down for in his will I was floored. I laughed it off and we joked, and when I hung up I got on with my day, and then it started to sink in. I don't want his stuff; I already got some stuff from him. There's the dresser that I use every day, a hand-me-down from his move to Dallas. A little paring knife, a gift from a trip to France, a shaving kit from another trip he made, and a birthday card every year that we've been friends. He showed me how to cook gourmet food and how to pick a wine, how to wear a tuxedo and impress the ladies. He shot an AK47 blank round off in the house one day, that's really loud. Diggs is the kind of person that has a party and every person gets along and meets a new friend. He finds strays and brings them into the fold. He takes care of things that you don't think need taking care of, but once they are you can't imagine how you did it before. Diggs has so much confidence that it spills over onto the rest of us.

Well, I could go on a lot longer but I know you have things to take care of. I just thought you should know that you've touch my life in infinite ways and whenever and wherever you are, you are not alone. You carry thoughts and prayers and good wishes from the thousands of people's lives you've touch over the years. Anytime you feel isolated or separated remember this letter and know you're not alone. Thanks hero, and by the way the only thing that you can will me is your life because I can't use anything of yours more than I can use you.

> *Love,*
> *Your "Brother",*
> *Bernie*

04 AUG 2002

Dear Friends and Family,

As of the 19th I will no longer be on AOL e-mail. Please use cptdiggs@hotmail.com. For regular mail, please use:

Bob Diggs Brown, Jr.
Unit 3c
APO AE 09354

When using regular mail, expect three weeks delivery time. Also, do not send anything until after October 1. I've heard that we will be very limited to e-mail access, so please, no mass mailings to my address. Now being a bit of a hypocrite, I, on the other hand, will be using mass mailings. ☺

I guess I'm about as ready as ever for this adventure. I've fired so many rounds through my carbine that I have a black and blue shoulder and a blister on my trigger finger. Our unit actually fired more rounds in the time we were at Fort Carson than the entire post fired all year! I think we are all pretty good marksmen at this point. We have the best equipment, best training, and highly motivated soldiers. You ought to see some of the equipment. I wish I could go into detail, but that might be an operational security violation.

Thanks for all the words of encouragement that you have sent in the past few weeks. Your thoughts mean a lot to me. I truly feel that we are at a defining moment in the history of our country. It is going to be my privilege to serve in the Armed Forces and contribute to the betterment of our society and the world as a whole.

An interesting item: Did you know that Afghanistan is 11½ hours ahead of Mountain Standard Time Zone? We will be over 7,500 nautical miles away!

I do have a couple of favors to ask:

For the folks at my bank, please feel free to share this information with anyone who might be interested. I will miss working with you guys and would love to continue to hear about your successes.

To anyone living in Duncan, Oklahoma, please keep an eye on my folks. They are really up there in age, and Mom is not taking this well at all.

Sincerely,

Diggs

21 AUG 2002

Dear Friends:

Things are moving right along here, and currently I'm about a week out from deploying overseas. Our training has been intense both in level and tempo. We finally got most of our desert-patterned gear (I was missing boots), and now the order of the day is packing 20 pounds of stuff into a 10-pound bag. The remaining gear that we are missing should come in at any moment. We will begin palletizing the majority of our gear today for the flight to Afghanistan.

You know, there are days when I can't believe that this is happening. I think when activation occurs it is much like a traumatic event. The reservist goes through an acceptance process much the same as the four phases of grieving:

1) Denial
2) Anger
3) Bargaining
4) Acceptance/rationalization

The defining moment for me was the day we were to report for active duty at our armory, which lies in an open field near Denver International Airport. The building can be seen from over a mile away. I recall the drive as non-eventful, much like any of the hundreds I've made to the same location. When I topped the first low-lying hill two miles away, I could see the antenna array near our headquarters. At this point I didn't give my fate much thought; this was the drive I'd made before. As I turned onto the dirt road for the final quarter mile, the full armory came into view with its parking lot perimeter lined with military trucks acting as a blockade against any potential terrorist preemptive

5

strike. I stopped my car and sat there for a few moments. Gathering my thoughts, I placed the car back into drive and pulled up to the gate. Guards were at the entrance checking identification. The thought that immediately came to mind was, "This is for real." At that point I had accepted my fate.

I know a lot of the men here are currently going through the same process as I have described—all of them in a different stage. The majority have accepted the inevitable. Last night we had a service to commemorate the event that has led us all to this destination—September 11. This service was led by our chaplain along with several of the command staff. I was asked to create and present a slide show that focused on the events of that ill-fated day. We held the ceremony at the old theater on the post. There are approximately 250 men in our battalion, and all were there dressed in desert camouflage. As to be expected when you have a gathering of "brothers," there were conversations, joking, discussions of the day's training, and horseplay.

When it came time for the service, the lights dimmed and the auditorium stilled. A sense of seriousness befell the audience. The operations officer began the ceremony with a few words and was followed by the chaplain asking everyone to share a few thoughts with their neighbor about where they were that fateful day last year. My presentation was next and was followed by the commander's speech and battalion reciting in unison the Special Forces Creed and Prayer. This was a very emotional experience, which I believe brought focus to all and acceptance to those who had not yet made that leap.

Well, that's it for now. We leave in the next two days. I shall miss all of you.

Sincerely,
Diggs

THE SPECIAL FORCES CREED

I am an American Special Forces Soldier! A professional!
I will do all that my nation requires of me.
I am a volunteer, knowing well the hazards of my profession.
I serve with the memory of those who have gone before me:
Roger's Rangers,
Francis Marion,
Mosby's Rangers,
The 1st Special Service Force,
The Jedburgs,
Detachment 101,
And the Special Forces soldiers
who have served their country in Vietnam.

I pledge to uphold the honor and integrity of all these,
in all that I am, in all that I do.
I am a professional soldier.
I will teach and fight wherever my nation requires,
liberating the oppressed.
I will strive always to excel in every art and artifice of war.

I know that I will be called upon to perform tasks in isolation,
far from familiar faces and voices.
With the help and guidance of my God,
I will conquer my fears and succeed.
I will keep my mind and body clean, alert and strong,
for this is my debt to those who depend on me.
I will not fail those whom I serve.
I will not bring shame upon myself or the Forces.
I will maintain myself, my arms and my equipment in an
immaculate state as befits a Special Forces Soldier.
I will never surrender though I be the last.
If I am taken, I pray that I have the strength to resist my enemy.
My goal is to succeed in any mission—and live to succeed again.
I am a member of my nation's chosen soldiery.
God grant that I may not be found wanting,
that I will not fail this sacred trust.

7

THE SPECIAL FORCES PRAYER

Almighty God,

Who art the Author of liberty and the Champion of the oppressed,

hear our prayer.

We, the men of Special Forces,

acknowledge our dependence upon Thee

in the preservation of human freedom.

Go with us as we seek to defend the defenseless

and to free the enslaved.

May we ever remember that our nation,

whose motto is "In God We Trust",

expects that we shall acquit ourselves with honor,

that we may never bring shame upon our faith, our families,

or our fellow men.

Grant us wisdom from Thy mind, courage from Thine heart,

strength from Thine arm, and protection by Thine hand.

It is for Thee that we do battle,

and to Thee belongs the victor's crown.

For Thine is the kingdom, and the power and the glory, forever.

AMEN

CHAPTER 2
OCONUS (Outside Continental United States)

Hey Brother,
I just want to say that my thoughts will be with you all the time and that I am very proud of my brother. I know that everything will be fine but difficult. Will be speaking about you all the time and make sure that Matt and Margaux will be so proud of you when you be back.
Good luck brother and will address all our prayers to you.

Pascal

26 AUG 2002

Dear Friends and Family:

Our flight arrived in Kabul around 4:00 in the morning. We'd been flying all night, having left Frankfurt, Germany, at 8:00 p.m. The flight was long, we ate cold sandwiches, the toilet filled to over capacity, and the interior of the aircraft was uncomfortably cool. The air crew consisted of National Guardsmen who had been activated for the war. They flew the C-17, the latest in the inventory designed to carry the heaviest battle tanks and replace the ever faithful C-130 Hercules.

The hull of the C-17 is like a cavern. We had a large truck, two trailers, and four pallets of gear in her belly. The 20 or so of us who rode along had to find room to stretch out on the cold aluminum floor and nap as we could. Some, who had planned ahead, brought their ground pads to sleep on. I wasn't one of those and the hard, cold flooring made sleep a challenge.

I had the privilege of riding in the cockpit of the carrier during an in-air refueling. At 22,000 feet we rendezvoused with a KC-135 tanker just before midnight. What a sight; we were less than 50 feet away from the tanker, and its fuel line was extended and feeding our plane hundreds of pounds of fuel per second. It was like a slow dance as the pilots maneuvered their aircraft into position. It seemed as if one could almost reach out and touch the observer who controlled the fuel line from the tanker. In the full moonlight, his oxygen-masked face was visible through the observation port. The moon lit up the blanket of clouds some 10,000 feet below us. The stars and the pitch-black sky surrounded the cockpit, and unbelievably, at least to me, the flight was silent. It was such a peaceful experience on the way to war.

As we approached our landing strip at Kabul International Airport (which is ironically abbreviated KIA), the main concern of the air crew was that the enemy had shoulder-fired missiles capable of knocking our plane out of the sky. There was also our apprehension of what awaited us on the ground after the flight. Just prior to landing, the crew chief gave out instructions over the loudspeaker that we were to move away from the aircraft and form a defensive perimeter in case we drew fire once we were on the ground.

The landing went without a hitch. As soon as the ramp was lowered, we moved off of the aircraft to form our perimeter in the darkness. Our greeting party pulled up in a bus and distributed ammunition and body armor, ours still being on pallets on the aircraft. The Turks who were running the ISAF (International Security and Assistance Force) Air Field had front-end loaders to remove our pallets, and this was quickly done. Our trailers and trucks were driven off of the aircraft. As soon as we were unloaded, the aircraft roared to life and departed for Germany.

It was first light—the period prior to the sunrise when your eyes can just begin to make out shapes. The mountains surrounding KIA are jagged and steep. Their silhouette reminded me a bit of Colorado, my home; but as the sun began to rise, it was apparent that we were in a war-torn country very far from Colorado. Destroyed aircraft littered the surrounding area. The terminal had been taken over by the Turks for use as

headquarters, and camouflage netting settled over everything—
not so much for concealment but for protection from the burning
sun that would be appearing soon.

Dawn broke and our bus pulled out of the terminal and into
what appeared to be a very poor neighborhood. The dirt streets
were lined with mud and mud-brick homes. Children were
already up pumping water from the wells that stood every few
blocks. The men squatted in groups sipping their tea and
exchanging tales. Women were nowhere to be seen. As I
eventually learned, what I believed to be a poor neighborhood
was actually typical.

The Afghanis turned with inquisitive eyes to watch as we
passed in our bus and armored Hummers, which kicked up an
enormous amount of dust. My thoughts were of all the times this
country had been invaded in the past. There was the possibility
that these people were only wondering who was passing through
at this point in history. We drove through the outskirts of Kabul
to our base on the far eastern side of town. An uneasiness filled
the bus as we diligently watched our surroundings, none of us
knowing what lay ahead. Many of us, myself included, kept our
thumbs on the safety of our rifles. Because most of us were
experiencing our first combat tour, you could cut the tension with
a knife.

The bus passed the main ISAF compound. ISAF is composed
of 24 nations on "peace keeping" operations. Multinational flags
flew outside the headquarters that was partially hidden by a
high and heavily guarded wall. The flags seemed to give the
garrison a circus-like appearance—much different from our
compound, as I would soon see.

A few hundred meters farther down the road, we pulled into
our compound. It is now called KMTC (Kabul Military Training
Center). It had once been a Soviet base and was built 15 or so
years ago. Due to occupation by the Taliban at the beginning of
the war, our Air Force had bombed it. Many of the buildings
were in ruin. Here there wasn't a PX (Post Exchange), air

conditioning, hot showers, or paved roads. Outhouses lined the end of the buildings, plywood covered the blown-out windows, and dust was everywhere. I really can't complain, though. I had lived in worse conditions on previous missions, but never for the length of time we were looking at here.

Active duty Special Forces had come into this compound several months before our arrival and had begun training the Afghan National Army (ANA). With their free time and nothing else to do, they had made many improvements to the facility. To them it had been home for the past six months, but now they were ready to go home and turn over the property to the new landlords, or should I say "slum lords"?

Due to lack of funds and aircraft for their travel home, Active Duty and National Guard got to spend the next few weeks together. There were over 500 men on a compound that could barely hold 300. Conditions were cramped, to say the least. Our unit was crammed temporarily into several overcrowded rooms, literally living on top of one another.

01 SEP 2002

As you probably realize with our limited e-mail access, whenever there is a line of others waiting to use the e-mail, my letters are short and to the point. When time permits, they will be of more length, and since there isn't much to do with our limited free time, I will compose even longer thoughts on my computer and download to e-mail. Such are the thoughts that follow.

When you look at Afghanistan it is hard to imagine it once was a much-sought-after resort destination. Amazing what 20-something years of war can do to a country. Kabul, the capital, has over 700,000 people, and the poverty level is overwhelming. The city occupies the main approach to the Khyber Pass, which links Afghanistan with Pakistan. As in Mexico, in Afghanistan you don't dare drink the water or eat off of the local economy.

The guys who have accidentally used water for even the simplest task (such as brushing teeth) have become violently ill. It should go without saying that we wash our hands all the time. I'm actually holding back on the temptation to buy a soda, which is available down the street. I am going to see if I can go the entire tour without. We have plenty of bottled water, boxed milk, and coffee in our mess hall. I should also mention that we are not allowed any alcoholic beverages while deployed, and that's not a bad thing.

The majority of the streets are dirt and gravel with massive potholes and lined with bombed-out ruins. The dwellings that are not bombed out are inhabited at a primitive level. Bombed out or not, as far as I can tell, every building has some sort of war-related damage. The main construction material here is mud brick. The homeowners who have real estate usually have a mud wall of approximately six feet in height surrounding them to protect their meager lot. Electricity is scarce, as is the running water. At night you can clearly see all the stars because there isn't the light pollution that you normally have in major cities.

The poor burn trash to keep warm. Sometimes, even at our location, you can see the haze of burning trash hanging over the city and smell the sickly sweet odor. Running water is a luxury that only a very few have, along with indoor toilets. In Colorado the higher you live on the mountain, the richer you are. Not so in Afghanistan; the folks who live up the mountain must go down to the well or river to get their water and haul it back up to their homes. Hand-pumped wells are every few blocks. Children have the task of collecting the morning water, and you will see them daily pumping and filling water buckets. Women are rarely seen on the street, and when they are, most wear the burka that covers them from head to toe. I hear that on the weekends some come to the market dressed in a more Westernly fashion, but have yet to see that myself. I did see one lady who was wearing a blue sequined burka and high heels!

Children begin their day pumping water for the family.

Along any street there are vendors, sometimes herds of goats, donkeys pulling carts, camels, and children playing. The traffic is limited. There are very few privately owned vehicles. There are, however, many overcrowded taxis and buses. The truck drivers use large lorries painted ornately with pictures of what must be paradise in their minds, as I haven't seen any landscape that resembles the art. The trucks are laughingly called "jingle trucks" due to the painted bright colors and the musical shards of metal that hang by chains from all points. The sound of car horns is persistent, the trash is abundant, and the air pollution is a constant irritant to both eyes and throat.

Some of the scenes I observe remind me of the old American westerns: dusty streets, horses, goats, children running about, gunslingers.... Did I say gunslingers? There aren't so many carrying guns in Kabul as there are in the smaller towns, but we do still see the firearms and do have to watch our backsides.

The people are very friendly and will attempt to communicate with us in their broken English. There are so many different dialects: Pashtun, Dari, Tajik, etc. The educated have higher language skills, and their English is passable. The majority of our interpreters are college educated. Many have been doctors, pilots, former military, and lawyers. They make more money working for us than they can at their old professions, and that isn't much. These poor guys occasionally get threats against them and their families for assisting us, but they know that in the long run a stable government for them will be a benefit.

I have compassion for the people of this country. It will be generations, if ever, before Afghanistan recovers from the devastation and becomes a modern society. They are their own worst enemies with the constant tribal feuds and blood debts. The Taliban and the fundamental Islamics have also made it a point to keep them in the Dark Ages. It is much easier to control the uneducated.

There are a couple of small villages close to our compound. Both villages have schools that are in desperate need of supplies. We've donated a few basic supplies, and for this they are very thankful. It all goes back to "winning the hearts and minds" of the populace. I have received a couple of handwritten letters from school kids in Colorado. They have each asked, "If there is anything you need, ask and we will send." I am going to suggest that the 6th grade class in Colorado adopt the 6th grade class here and send supplies. I will get this coordinated with our chaplain in the near future, another project to occupy my time. Chaplain Andy and I will also be teaching English once a week until school lets out in the winter. We have made this our project, the chaplain taking the initiative and asking my help.

The Taliban, as you know, was the previous government of this country. They came to power by force and with backing by Iran and Pakistan. Some of the Taliban were Mujahedeen who fought the Soviet occupation. The Taliban were very brutal, yet almost laughable in their rule. Most, being illiterate, had no concept of appeasing the populace in exchange for support. They took control of Afghanistan and implemented a rule designed to eliminate the "evil Western influence" and bring Islam and culture back to Year One. The United States being called the

"Great Satan" for years by Islamic fundamentalists should have been our first clue that the terror attacks were going to occur.

The Taliban had a plan to restore their version of order to Afghanistan, which basically was to take Afghanistan back to Year One and restart their version of civilization. The Year One concept was designed to initiate fundamental Islamic values in society. The Taliban came up with such absurd laws as:

1) Kite flying (national pastime of Afghan children) is illegal. Those who fly kites will be punished.

2) All men must grow beards. Men who do not will be punished.

3) Women must be covered from head to toe. If they leave the house unescorted by their husband or a male relative, the husband will be punished.

4) Raising birds (pigeons are a favorite pet here) is illegal. All birds will be killed and the owner punished.

5) Women's shoes must not make noise.

6) No artwork allowed.

7) No music allowed.

8) No phones allowed.

9) Women don't go to school.

10) No photos, sculptures, drawings, or any representation of humans or animals.

11) Women who commit adultery or premarital sex will be stoned to death.

The list goes on and on. The Taliban enforced these laws with public executions, beatings, and amputations. They are very archaic in their thoughts and actions. Amazingly enough, the Taliban is still supported by Islamic fundamentalists in Pakistan and surrounding areas where madrasas (religious schools) still teach the youth to hate Christians and all things Western. The children graduate from these schools once they have memorized the 6,346 verses of the Koran. They're not taught how to use computers or any of the other modern technologies that our children grow up with.

The Soviets, during their occupation, treated the people better than the Taliban had, but not by much. They were ruthless in fighting the Mujahedeen and punished those who supported the rebels. Poison gas was a common weapon used on the populace. Torture was used to get information, by both sides. The Mujahedeen were also ruthless with the Russians, very rarely sparing any prisoners. Cutting the throat was the common form of execution by the Mujahedeen, often videotaped and sent to Soviet news agencies. When the Soviets were defeated at Bagram, the 300 prisoners were beheaded and their heads were placed about Bagram. The headless torsos were dumped in a large open pit.

The forces we are facing now are comprised of Taliban, al Qaeda, Hizb-i-Islami (abbreviated as HIG), and an assortment of warlords who do not wish to lose their grip on power. Members of the HIG are such fundamentalists that even the Taliban will have nothing to do with them! The country is made up of tribes that are in a constant state of infighting. The bad guys have learned that they cannot go toe-to-toe with U.S. forces. Whenever they have massed, we have called in air strikes and killed many of their fighters, as you may have witnessed on television; i.e., Tora Bora and Operation Anaconda. Now they are resorting to small unit attacks and terrorism. Favorite terror targets are the shops that sell TVs and DVDs since these are clearly bringing in the Western influence. The killing of civilians by the enemy is an aspect I don't understand. They are undermining any popular support they might have had, but as I mentioned earlier, they aren't the brightest humans on the planet.

One of the problems we are having is discerning who the bad guys in town are; they blend in with the populace because they do not wear uniforms. Also, there are rewards offered by Taliban to locals who kill Americans. We do get information from time to time from the locals as to who the enemy might be. The majority of the populace does not want return of Taliban rule and they see us as liberators.

I have mentioned that the U.S. isn't the only country involved in "nation building" here. There is a conglomerate of European countries under the coalition name International Security Assistance Force (ISAF). They have a massive compound down the road that is like living at the Hilton compared to ours. They have such amenities as hot showers, pools, clubs, beer (you can't imagine how good a cold beer would taste now), women (in uniform), great food, air conditioning, heat, etc. It is almost like a "little Europe" there. Did I mention that we don't have a PX or anything of the sort on our tiny base?

Our compound, which was once occupied by Taliban, had all the electric lights ripped out, and different rooms were used indiscriminately as toilets—excrement is everywhere. They even built fires on the floors in the rooms! The compound is in disarray from neglect and combat damage. Primitive may be an understatement as to the quality of life here, although we do have intermittent electricity provided by generators. It is going to take a lot of work to get this place into shape. Right now we are practically living on top of one another until some of the other buildings are cleared and we can spread out.

A few days ago, several of us made the drive to Bagram where the United States has a major air base. It isn't far by distance, but it is far time-wise. The two-lane road to Bagram is in relatively good shape, as roads go in this country, and it winds through a desolate valley. The old road (commonly referred to as "Ambush Alley") winds through the passes, and as the name implies, it is a lethal thoroughfare. This is the road where the Soviet military used to get ambushed on a regular basis. There are plenty of burned-out hulks of trucks and tanks lining the way into Bagram.

Along the major roadways are checkpoints manned by the Northern Alliance soldiers and occasionally soldiers belonging to warlords. Their purpose is to regulate traffic and collect "tolls" from truckers. We blow through these checkpoints without a second thought, and the guards have no intention of delaying us. We do get a friendly wave, which is returned in kind.

Bedouin tents occasionally can be seen from the road, along with goat and camel herds. Also along this road are vast mine fields. You don't pull off the road for any reason. Afghanistan has over six million Soviet mines still in place. The fields that are cleared are marked with stones painted white. Mines fields waiting to be excavated are marked with stones painted red. It is amazing to see how many are still awaiting deactivation by friendly forces. What's even more amazing is to see the locals nonchalantly wandering in these areas. It is estimated that 10 people a day die from mines in Afghanistan. There is no telling how many more are wounded. Mines, after all, are designed to maim, not kill, because it takes two people to move a wounded soldier. Now three soldiers are out of the battle.

The valley into Bagram is stark. Afghanistan is into the fifth year of a drought. Every few miles there will be the remnants of a deserted mud-brick village. The farmers also have walled compounds about the size of football fields along the route and scattered throughout the valley. I'm assuming that this is a very common sight in this country. I have been told different purposes for these compounds: gathering places for clans, livestock pens, storage or fields for crops, and private property with a water well. The couple I have gotten close to contained vineyards. Whatever the purpose, they are formidable stockades, and there is no telling just how long some of them have been in existence. I should also mention that the sand and dirt here are khaki in color. Everything here is khaki. Note to self: Next trip to Afghanistan bring only khaki-colored clothing—dirt and dust everywhere.

In sharp contrast to the valley are the mountains that surround it. Here there are few foothills but many sheer and rugged mountains. They are spectacular in their appearance, snowcapped and piercing the clouds. The valley floor is at 6,500 feet above sea level, and I'm assuming that the peaks are easily over 17,000 feet. The mountains have no trees and very little vegetation on them—such a difference from the Rockies. This place reminds me of the moon, except for the people and the trash.

In the distance, at the base of the mountains there are green areas. This is where the villages are located and, of course, wherever there are villages, there is water. The water table is located at a shallow depth near the mountain base. I'm assuming that when there is rain, it must come down in torrents, as there are wadis (gullies) eight feet deep or more cutting jagged paths through the valley. These wadis are deep and wide enough to hide tanks and other large vehicles. Hulks of tanks litter the valley. I don't know if they are from the Soviet occupation, the recent war, or both.

Well, I must be moving on…things to do, people to meet. There are some big events coming up in the very near future.

I'm going to enclose some photos of things around town and in the country. I think they might be of interest.

Also, I want to make clear to those of you reading this material that I'm not whining. I think we have it pretty good compared to those who have gone before us. I have the utmost respect for the soldiers who have served our country in the past in much worse conditions than we face today. You should thank all veterans you see for the sacrifices they made and what they accomplished.

Thanks Dad, Paul, Jay, Bob, and all the rest.

Diggs

My father, Major Bob Diggs Brown, Sr., somewhere in Iraq during World War II. Sacrifices by him and men like him helped to keep America the Bastion of Freedom for the world.

My best friend, Paul Haubrich, in Vietnam. He is too young to drink beer but old enough to fight. His generation of warriors never got the "thank you" they deserved. Well, here it is: Thanks, Buddy!

21

CHAPTER 3
CORRESPONDING WITH THE CHILDREN

Here are some letters I received from grade school children from across the United Sates. To keep their thoughts pure, I haven't corrected their spelling or grammar.

Dear Soldier,

Thank you for protecting me, my family, and my friends. They are very imporent to me. I believe in you to protect our country. I know you have a lot of courage so keep protecting us more so we can have a good life and I hope you do too. Rember belive in your self and you can do it. I know you can. God loves you and others.

Dear My Specail Friend,

Thank you for protecting are country.

Dear Soldier,

I am real thankfull for all the good deeds you have done for us. I think you all are so brave. When the terrorist attacked I was really afraid, and when I saw tapes and videos about the bombings, I was also sad. Now I don't have to worry about that because you and all the other soldiers are protecting us. I am most thankfull for you trying your best to protet our nation. The wheather is cold around here, and the leaves are beautiful. Now I have some questions to ask. How is the wheather where you are? What kinds of foods do you eat? Have you seen any snakes, scropians, any kinds of bugs?

Dear Soldier,

Hi my name is Nancy, and Im so glad that you have the streanth and courage to go and fight for our country that proves that you car fore our country. And I hope that this war will be over soon so you may go back home to you wife and kids. It was realy bad thers a lot of killing in this world. But one day I hope their will be piece in all earth people. Im glad you ther right know and I'm sure Jesus Christ will watch over you and keep you in his hand and make sure you never get hurt. And I have faith and hope just like Jesus gave us. And a couple weeks ago it turned realy cold how is it down there? Do you have any pets? Do you tell stories? And do [you think] you are gonna win this war? Course I think you are couse I have fatih and I love you tho I don't know who I am talking to. But I love you.

Dear Soldier,

Thank you for fighting for our countrey. Some of yal has died and I'm so sorry. My uncle is in the marines and I miss him. And I know you miss your family to. I am so proud of you for fighting for our country so we can have freedom. My starts to cry a lot because some people have died. She sleeps with a picture of a soldier like you. What is it like to be at war? I know you don't like it because you have to sleep on the ground.

Dear Soldiers,

Thank you for fighting for America. We are thankful to you. That is nice of you to do that for us. Were sorry for what that mean mean man did to us.

Dear Soldiers,

I herd you are going into battle. I appresheate it. We are sinding you some goodies that we hope you like. We hate that you ar not going to be with your famliys this Chrsitmas. We also apresheate you going it battle for us. Frome your friends.

Dear Soldiers,

I hear you will not be with your family. We will bear goods and other things. I heard you are going into battle. We hope you will ben with your family of Chismas.

Dear Solders,

Thank you for protecting are country. Im sorry you had to go off to war without your family. I hope you are not very sad. So have a very merry Christmas.

Dear Soldier,

I bet your family misis you. I hope you get to come back soon and your family probly does to. They love you and care for you if you died I don't know what they would do. Be carefull.

Dear Soldier,

We are praying for you. You are keeping us safe. You have God on your side. No one cane beat God. So don't be fraid you can do it. And be careful, and brave. We hope you win. Put all you rmight in God. Hill help you.

Dear Soldier,

I am glad you are fighting for us to be free. I hope you can home soon to be with you family. Thank you for everything you do for us. I know how you feel the school that I went to got blew away in the storm last year. I fell sorry for you a lot.

Dear Solier

I go to elementary school. And I want to thank you for protecting are country. And fhating for freedom. I now it is verey hot our thar. And it is verey hard to staey away from your love one's. I now it is probly hard to sleep on the grownd. I am paring for you, but you now we are goning to win this fhite.

Dear Soldier,

I am sorry that you have to be cold. And I know you are over sea. But I can still send my love from Alabama to the state you are in.

Dear Soligers,
I like your guns but how do you get water and fud?

Dear Solders,
Thank you for helping us and our country and the united stats and you are gowing to win the war. My baseball teem is praying for you solders. I like to camp and go hikeing. What do you like to do?

Dear Soldier,
Thank you for surving for our country. You soldiers are the bravest people in this contry. Did you allways want to be a soldier? I want to be an actor. I write poems. I wrote a poem about America.

Dear Soilders,
I hope you like the stuff we are sinding you for Christmas. We are happy because you falaght for us. We love you. Do you need more stuff? We will send it to you. I want to be a soilder to.

Dear Amy & Tracy,

I am writing this letter to you simultaneously, but promise to write you as individuals in the future.

My name is Bob Diggs Brown, Jr. I go by the name Diggs because it is very distinctive. I am a captain in the U.S. Special Forces (Green Berets). I am 45 years old and live in Fort Collins, but at the moment I am in Afghanistan. I am not married and haven't any children, but someday, maybe. My hobbies are golf, hiking/camping, and entertaining friends.

I am a member of the Colorado Army National Guard. To be in the Guard means that you serve part time in the military. My unit has been activated to fight the war against terrorism, and I will be overseas for approximately one year.

In my civilian job I am a banker who sells stocks and bonds. I help people invest their money for growth and impending use. I love my job at the bank because it allows me to help people make decisions that will influence their future. I also like my military job that is making me part of history and also an influence on the future of our country.

I miss my family. My parents are very old, probably old enough to be your grandparents or great grandparents. I have three older sisters who live in Brazil, France, and Texas. One thing I would like to pass on to you is that you should tell your parents and close friends that you love them as often as you can.

The people we are fighting are very bad. They dislike America because we are a free society and almost everyone lives a good life. The Taliban (the bad government here in Afghanistan) did not allow TV, radio, art, and even kite flying. No music, no paintings—I can't imagine living like that. They wouldn't let girls go to school or even go outside unless each was covered head to toe in a burka and escorted by a male relative. Your teacher will probably have a picture of a burka to show you. The majority of the people in Afghanistan are glad we are here, but there still are bad guys who hate America, and we are fighting them.

Afghanistan is about the size of the state of Texas. It can be very hot here and it can also be very cold. It is dusty and the wind blows a lot. They have "dust devils" here. They are like miniature tornadoes made of dust. Every few days a sandstorm will pass through and you can't see very far at all due to the intensity of the storm.

Amy, I'm glad to hear that you plan on acting in your future. When I was younger I used to be on a television show called "Dallas." I only played bit parts, but my friends would call me sometimes and tell me that they'd seen me on television. It was a lot of fun. I see from your letter that you also write poems. Good for you! I used to write poetry myself, but have neglected such matters as of late. Maybe I'll find something to write about while I'm here. I would like to read your poem on America.

Tracy, who is your favorite baseball team? What position do you play? I enjoy hiking and camping also. I guess you've been to Estes Park and Rocky Mountain National Park. Beautiful places, aren't they?

Please tell your classmates that everyone here really appreciated the letters. One girl wrote a poem about patriots that has the lines "left, right, left, right...." It was very nice. Unfortunately, not all of the soldiers will be able to write back because we are extremely busy, and some people are just not good about writing letters. Letters take anywhere from one to three weeks to get home.

Well, I have to get back to work now. Both of you take care and study hard. Remember that you live in the greatest country that has ever existed.

Sincerely,
Diggs Brown

Dear Christopher,

Thank you for the letter. At the moment I am in Afghanistan in a city named Kabul. I used to live in Fort Collins where I worked for a bank before being called in to fight the war. Afghanistan has mountains a bit taller than the ones in Colorado, but there aren't any trees on them and there is little grass.

I appreciate your offer of sending me items I may need, but I have plenty of everything. The people in this country have very little. I wish there were a way to get gifts to them to make their lives easier. You are very lucky to live in America.

I am in the Army Special Forces (Green Berets). We jump out of airplanes and I have over 200 jumps. Many are free-fall, like you have seen at the Air Force Academy in Colorado Springs, but from a much higher altitude. We jump from such heights that we must wear oxygen masks to breathe and it is really cold.

I guess the most important thing I can tell you about jumping is to always keep your cool, know what you are doing, and don't be scared.

If you think you might want to join the military when you are older, that is a good thing. I would suggest that you join the Boy Scouts so you get an idea of what an orderly and challenging life is like. It can be a lot of fun and sometimes very hard.

Well, I have to get back to work now. Take care, mind your teacher and study hard. Remember that you live in the best country in the world.

Sincerely,
Diggs Brown

CHAPTER 4
HOME SWEET HOME

Hi Diggs,

You are a celebrity here at Worthington High School!

I shared the amazing gifts you sent (THANK YOU!!) with my students today. I read parts of your e-mail to Dave to the classes.

The students were somber as they listened to your heartfelt words and the Special Forces Creed. Thank you for helping us better understand what you and your comrades are doing there.

I'm so proud of you! And I'm very grateful that we met last April in Tucson and shared a few laughs.

Thank you very much for the unexpected package in yesterday's mail. I passed around the scarves and hats during class. Some students tried them on, trying to figure out how the items are worn. We'll all pay more attention to the news and news pictures of the war effort in Afghanistan and Pakistan.

I did, also, share your e-mail address with interested students. So if you are inundated with weird kid-speak e-mail, that's why.

I cautioned them to show you the respect you deserve, as you defend democracy in your dangerous mission.

We are praying for your safe return. Take care.

Cheryl

03 SEP 2002

Dear Friends,

Today I had the opportunity to go to the king's palace on a "hearts and minds" mission. Our battalion surgeon in the civilian world works as a pediatric eye surgeon. A couple of the OGA (other government agency) guys who guard the palace knew we had a quality medical staff and asked for help for a child who was having problems with his vision. The child was the son of an Afghan military officer who serves at the palace. The poor kid can't focus his wandering eyes on anything. Doc held out a piece of candy for the child and he couldn't even focus on the treat just a few inches in front of his face. After the exam, Doc explained to the father that his son would be legally blind his entire life, and that was that. The child's retinas had not developed. I know the father's heart was broken, but in this country the health standards are so poor that things like this are accepted. The doc said that even if the boy had lived in America, he still couldn't have done anything for him.

The palace itself is not in very good condition. It had been built in the 1920s, and even though the architecture was designed to appear antique, the war and neglect had not been good for it. While we didn't enter the formal section of the structure, what we did see was in disarray and damaged by the war. It is not at all like the palaces one might imagine from the Arabian Nights.

I would like to mention the health standards here. The average lifespan is 42.5 years. I've seen many people with at least one blind eye. Tuberculosis is rampant, as is malaria. There are large numbers of amputees out on the street. It seems there is an abundance of people here with crossed eyes. I wonder if this is the result of tribal inbreeding or a diet lacking proper nutrition.

04 SEP 2002

We've held a graduation for our first class of military trainees. It is amazing to see the transformation from feuding tribesmen to a united force that is the result of sweating together. There was plenty of press coverage from around the world. CNN, Newsweek, Time, and NBC were here, along with Al Jazeera (the very biased Arab network), and others. As Americans, we have to be successful in this mission. The entire Arab world is watching. If we fail here, our children and great grandchildren will suffer the consequences.

Something to note, the bad guys here are mostly Arab, Chechen, Yemeni, and Pakistani. Very few of the terrorists are actually Afghanis. Most of the Afghan people are happy that we are here. We have brought back prosperity and lifted them out of the Stone Age.

The soldiers we are training come from all over the country to join. They are of different tribes: Tajiks, Pashtuns, Hajiks, etc. Some come primarily for the money, which isn't much. I like to think that most of them come for the good of the country. I believe that a few years under Taliban rule have finally convinced these people that they must put their tribal differences behind them. The screening process is intense because we don't want infiltrators within the unit.

We are not alone in this process of getting the new Afghan army up to combat status. Countries from all over the world donate supplies to assist. Typically we wind up getting the surplus material from countries such as Germany, Spain, Poland, and a number of other European nations. The supplies are just trickling in at the moment, barely enough to keep things going. Most of the munitions are from former Soviet block countries. This makes our training a bit more interesting. We have to learn the weapon system ourselves before we can teach it to the Afghan soldiers.

06 SEP 2002

A few days ago three of us went downtown with our interpreter. We visited a shopping area named Chicken Street. It is the Afghan equivalent of 5th Avenue in New York City, but not at all glamorous, believe me! It is only five blocks long, very congested, and dirty. Traffic control is nonexistent. There weren't many tourists, and those who were there were from the embassies or other agencies, all wearing body armor. While we weren't shopping, per se, we did stop in a couple of shops as we walked down the street. What a peculiar feeling, wearing armor, carrying weapons, and covering each other from opposite sides of the street.

The hot items to buy here are rugs, old rifles, and antiques. I'm checking out the rifles at this moment. They were manufactured by Tower in the mid 1800s, in pretty good shape, and sell for about $300. I checked the Internet and they are selling at auction for $2,000 to $5,000. I may have to buy one or two. I will also pick up a rug before I come home.

The active duty guys have been departing for home over the past few days. I know they are excited to be leaving. Their disappointment is very evident when a flight out is delayed. I can't imagine what is going through their minds, but I am sure at some point I will know personally.

We finally were able to move into our permanent quarters, thus giving a bit of room (not much) to spread out. I went around to all the scrap piles of wood and gathered enough to make a bed that is raised off the floor so I can store my locker and duffle bags underneath. I made the "bed project" a focus for a couple of days to help pass time. It is about four feet off the ground with a ladder, headboard, footboard, and carvings created with a jigsaw. It is the envy of the camp. My little hovel was like a parade of homes, everyone stopping in to admire (or mock) the craftsmanship.

One of the other things I have done here to pass time is to set up "The Fabulous Bombay Lounge." It is nothing more than a large wooden sign I cut out of plywood using a jigsaw, and a couple of aluminum-loading pallets as the floor. It sits out in the courtyard. Every Thursday night I show a DVD movie "under the stars" using a projector and speaker system. It can get a bit dusty at times and very cold by the end of the movie, but everyone bears with it. It is a nice break, and Friday is our day off. We start the evening with a Sinatra CD, then we go to a short Monty Python video, and finally the feature presentation. Everyone brings their own chair and water. Of course, cigars are all around (while they last), and we have popcorn. If only the lounges were this nice back home!

We can buy knock-off DVDs here, including the most recent movies within days of their release—some even before their release! They cost one dollar and only a very few are of good quality. Most appear to have been filmed by someone holding a video camera while seated in a theatre. We will actually see people walking in front of the screen, hear them talking, and see the camera jiggle. It is too comical! It reminds me of something I saw on "Seinfeld" once.

Must run now. I miss all of you.

Diggs

The Fabulous Bombay Lounge. Though not an actual structure, the FBL was more a state of mind, providing a much needed morale boost during trying times.

CHAPTER 5
WINNING THE HEARTS AND MINDS

Dear Diggs,

I'm mighty proud of you, my friend, and have told damn near everyone who will stand still long enough about your fine commitment to our beloved country. One thing occurred to me after your e-mail... I remember having to watch the kids very closely for grenades, small pistols and glass in Cokes. I know your situation is very different, but exploiting children is a favorite of our enemy.

Ask me for anything you need and I'll make it so.

Paul, SP/5 Runnoft

Dear Diggs,

Your most recent letter was very touching and we feel that we can be of assistance and further create well-being among the locals. My wife works at a dental office and is able to buy boxes of large quantities of toothbrushes and tubes of toothpaste. The toothpaste isn't the small variety, but she is checking on that. Nevertheless, I'm sure they can be used by families with many members, or for that matter anyone who needs toothpaste. Please give me an idea what would be best as far as school supplies are concerned, a monetary donation or the supplies themselves, such as a gross of pencils or spiral notebooks. I am sure that you know what is the route to take for the most "bang for the buck."

Your letters really touched me, Diggs, and I am continually amazed at your altruistic, unselfish motivation. Not that I would have perceived you any other way, as Di has always portrayed you as a very special person. I guess I had no idea of the far reaching compassion of the warrior/soldier, who is frequently portrayed as an aggressor not a humanitarian, and I am doing as much as possible to correct the image which has been unfairly labeled on the members of the soldiers of the world involved in rebuilding the "A". I must say that in the short time I have known you, in cyberspace at that, I feel a sense of "Christian brotherhood and love" with you. I would really like to, above all, thank you for clearing up the misconceptions that existed between my perceived reality and the truth. YOU ARE A ONE IN A BILLION PERSON! GOD BLESS YOU AND YOUR FELLOW AMBASSADORS OF PEACE, FOR WHAT YOU ARE DOING!!!!!

Sincerely,
David and Susan

Wherever we travel children follow us, flash a thumbs up and shout "Thank you America, thank you George Bush!"

08 NOV 2002

Dear Friends and Family,

Today Chaplain Andy and I went to Pol-e-charkhi School to meet the superintendent. Pol-e-charkhi is a small village near our compound that is populated by about 2,000 people. Every time we drive into the village, the children come out and enthusiastically surround our vehicle, giving us the thumbs up and saying, "Thank you!" The chaplain (I've nicknamed him Rabbi) and I will be teaching English at the school, and we will only teach the boys. The Afghanis will not allow us to teach the girls. They won't even allow the girls and the boys to attend any classes together. To them it is really not a priority to have the girls in class; in fact, the Taliban forbade it.

We begin classes tomorrow, once a week, and gradually will move to two times a week. I won't make it every day as I will be out doing other things that the military deems more mission-essential. One of the benefits of our helping the school is that many of the locals who want us to stay and educate their children will give us information on the bad guys. I will be armed at all times. Imagine teaching class while wearing a pistol and having a carbine within arm's reach!

The school is actually four buildings with a dirt play yard. (Have I mentioned the enormous amount of dirt and dust in this country?) Very little grass is growing in Afghanistan at the moment due to the drought. All the windows in the school have been blown out from fighting, and the Taliban, who want the people to remain ignorant, broke out all the lights and chalkboards. The rooms are bare—no furniture, little chalk, no heat, no air, and no glass in the windows. The chalkboards are no more than an area on the wall or a board painted black. No erasers. The students sit on rugs that they bring to school every day. The classes are crowded, and the children are eager to learn.

Let me mention something about the dirt/dust in this country. There have been five to seven years of severe drought. The dust resembles talcum powder. Every step you take kicks up a cloud of dust. It reminds me of Pigpen in the *Peanuts*® cartoon strip. Our vehicles have to have their filters changed constantly, and it is impossible to keep our weapons clean. We do not oil our weapons in order to prevent them from jamming with the dust-caked oil. All the computers are going on the fritz, and very few have working CD-ROMs or A: drives. I keep my personal computer in a carrying case when not in use. No one, and I mean no one, has clean clothes. Whenever civilians wear their version of business suits (although very few wear them), they are caked in dust. A lot of the items I have brought with me will remain here because they will never come clean again, and the electronics will not be functional when it is time to go home.

09 SEP 2002

Chaplain Andy and I taught our first classes today. The classes went over extremely well with very enthusiastic students. Since there isn't any glass in the windows, students not assigned to the class came to listen in. Sometimes the teachers shooed them off with small stones, sticks, or harsh words. I got a great photo of a little girl sticking her head in the window to check out the class. Her name is Farista. She is the daughter of the school's custodian. She stood outside the window all day.

Farista intently listens in on the boys' English lesson. She came every Wednesday to eavesdrop, as the girls had no class to attend at this point in time.

We started class with the ABC song and worked our way through greetings. The day went fast as we taught five 40-minute classes. The classes ranged in size from 8 to 60 students. The grades are not separated by age, but by knowledge. Since the Taliban had pretty much dismantled the school system, there were students ranging from 11 years old to 26 years old mixed together in the classes. The Taliban has pretty much given Afghanistan a generation of illiterates, and it will be years before this country ever recovers from that insanity.

The students are going to school under difficult conditions. They have nothing except what we have given them. It is pitiful. Pens are the hot item. Notebooks are also welcomed gifts for these kids. Many of the children literally walk miles to come to school. Most of them are barefoot.

After our first day of class, the teachers invited us to stay at their homes for dinner, but we politely refused. As I mentioned earlier, we must be careful about what we eat and drink. Also, there is a security issue. Even though we are close to our base, there is still danger around every corner.

About the population, there are many different ethnicities in the children and their parents due to the enormous amount of armies that have occupied this country over the years. Some look very Russian, others Mongolian, some Arab, and some European. I think the Russian features are the most predominant with the children's age groups we are teaching.

13 SEP 2002

We had a bit of excitement very early this morning. Just around 2:00 a.m. several rockets impacted nearby. Fortunately no one was hurt. It did make it very difficult to get back to sleep with all the adrenalin flowing. Some of us didn't get back to sleep with the higher state of alert and extra guards posted just in case the enemy attempted to breach our perimeter. This is the first time we have been fired upon. It is not at all like you see in the movies. The buildings shake, items on the shelf fall, and there is a bit of confusion. I think we handled the situation quite well for the first encounter.

If you are of the mind that we shouldn't go into Iraq and eliminate Saddam and his cronies, you'd better think again. We are dealing with some evil people who would like nothing better than to slaughter you, your family, and your friends. This is their intent and their goal. Saddam is just a small piece of the puzzle, but this small piece has the capability to deliver a devastating weapon into the hands of the terrorists he backs. We can go all over the world putting out fires, or we can stop them at the source; we can fight them on their home turf, or we can wait for another 9/11 and fight them on our doorstep.

The Taliban have made it a habit of giving out toy guns to the children in hopes that a soldier might mistake it for a real gun. The result would be a child being shot, which would create an incident that could be used as propaganda against us. Some of the toy guns are exact replicas of real guns and have all of the functions, except firing capability. A young boy pointed a toy gun at me yesterday. I caught the movement out of the corner of my eye and instantly turned to fire on what appeared to be an impending threat. Looking through my sights, I saw the smiling face of a very young boy. I had the presence of mind not to fire, and I'm not ashamed to admit that it did startle me quite a bit.

The Taliban also murder children (females) who attend school. They have no concept of the value of human life. They look at you and me, and anyone else who doesn't fit their mold, as nothing more than vermin that must be destroyed. I find it hard to believe that there are people of this ilk in the world, but there are, and we must deal with them effectively and immediately. I find it even harder to believe that there are people who blame our country for the evils of the world and side with these sick bastards. The President was correct when he said, "You are either with us or with the terrorists."

There are a lot of things going on in the world that I cannot go into detail with you, but maybe someday. I will tell you that the terror threat should be on the forefront of our nation's agenda. We are truly in an undeclared world war that it is just at the infancy stage. You will soon see terrorist organizations around the world that follow the hateful and irrational Islamic fundamentalist cause. The terrorist organizations will not be strongly linked, but united in a common cause—to destroy all things Western and our way of life. They will be seeking weapons of mass destruction to rain death on as many Americans as possible in hopes of devastating our resolve to be free. Most likely they are going to be supported by "shadow governments" within the hierarchy of countries—some we consider our allies, and some are obvious enemies. Other allies will bow to the terrorist pressure; they have no resolve for freedom, many having their roots deeply planted in a socialist system. There will be no negotiations with these harbingers of death; they have nothing to gain from peace. To believe any differently is naivety at its worst. If we, as a nation, lose focus on this war and put other political agendas ahead of it, we are going to see devastation on our own soil, the likes of which have never been witnessed here before. I don't mean to scare anyone; it's just my opinion, for what it is worth. I'll hop off my soapbox.

16 SEP 2002

I was assigned to teach map reading classes to the Afghan army officers. Today I held my first class. Many of the officers had not even seen a compass. Of these soldiers, some have been fighting for years as the Mujahedeen against the Russians and Taliban. These veterans have some horrendous stories to tell.

The classroom we used was in a two-story building that had serious damage, like all the others. We were able to find plastic patio furniture (much like you buy in the States) to furnish the room. I got up to the room a couple of hours prior to the class and swept out the years of dust and broken glass, and then I set up the furniture. I also found six 100-foot extension cords to run from our compound to this classroom so that I could use my computer and projector. The students had never seen a projector, and very few had seen a laptop computer. They were very interested in the technology.

My classes went extremely well, and I have been asked to present more subject matter in the future. I get along very well with my interpreters and students, even though my jokes don't always translate. I am trying to learn Dari now. I started on Pashtun, but as it turns out, in this region Dari is prevalent. My interpreter, Tem, is 24 and teaches English on his own in town. He is a good kid. I hope that he visits America someday.

I've had several of y'all ask if you can send anything. We pretty much have everything we need. What I have needed personally, Marcia, Lanna, Mom and Dad, and Paul have sent. A couple of quality cigars would be nice; those we can't get. We can get most small items at the PX at Bagram Air Force Base when we can get up that way. The line to get into the PX takes at least an hour, and then you have about another 20 minutes to check out. We make it to the PX about every three weeks. Selection is not great, but the essentials are there.

I do have a request, if you are looking for something to send. For the kids in my class at Pol-e-charkhi, if any of you could send colored chalk, white chalk, blackboard erasers, Denver Bronco posters, periodic table chart, anatomy chart, small Colorado flags, world atlas, or a map of the States. Those would be greatly appreciated. These kids have absolutely nothing. They walk sometimes miles to the school, literally barefoot and in all types of weather. Only the lucky few have a pencil and notepad. Some do have backpacks, but these are scarce and I'm not really sure what they are carrying in the pack. I can tell you, it is not school supplies.

Please note address change:
Bob Diggs Brown, Jr.
Unit 20 N
APO, AE 09354

We wash our clothes by hand, or when we have electricity we use some dilapidated washers on our compound that take two hours to cycle. The dryers do not spin; they bake the clothes dry. When line-drying laundry, our clothes are caked in dust by the time they eventually dry. For the most part, showers are cold— when we have them. This winter will be interesting because we have no heat. I sealed my windows with foam sealant and plywood and thought I did a good job, but last night's sandstorm filled my room. I will try and figure out another way to solve this dilemma. The problem is that we have plywood where the glass should be. I also have a large rocket-generated hole in the roof over my bed that lets in copious amounts of sand and cold air. I guess I should be thankful it doesn't rain here.

One of the enemies on our compound is bacteria. The Afghanis, for the most part, defecate on the ground pretty much anywhere that suits them. Centuries of this (along with the drought) has produced a fine dust that is filled with bacteria. When we first arrived here many of us were battling lung infections from inhaling this dust. Other things to be wary of are gastro-intestinal problems and sinus infections. Constant hand washing is a must. The flies that have been dining on the piles of dung have pretty much died off as the nights have become colder. There is a bright side to winter setting in!

We have three Air Force guys here who are our "weathermen." Their daily briefing is pretty much the same, "High of 75°, low of 38°, dust, haze, winds of 5 to 7 knots increasing as evening falls; no precipitation." If you know anything about the Air Force you will know that, for the most part, they are not accustomed to the squalor we are living in. I will admit that these three are taking everything in stride. They are a jovial bunch—National Guard, also. Their tour is almost up and it is evident that they are ready to go home.

We showed the movie "Lawrence of Arabia" tonight at the Fabulous Bombay Lounge. It was so appropriate with the sand blowing, the desert sky, the full moon, and camels nearby. I felt like I was right there with Peter O' Toole fighting the Turkish army. I might mention that the Bombay Lounge has doubled in size; we now have four pallets, and the participation has really picked up. I have also had an embroidery company in Florida, *Jasmine Designs*, create Bombay Loungewear to include tee-shirts and hats. The big question I now hear around the compound is, "What is the movie Thursday?"

18 SEP 2002

I've started coordinating missions with the European (ISAF) units. They are here on a "peace keeping" mission, while the U.S. is training the Afghan army and performing combat missions. It is important that we keep out of each other's way, yet still support the other. The French gave me a baguette this afternoon—ah, heaven! The Germans are quite pleasant and efficient, as expected. All the foreign officers speak English, and this makes the meetings much easier to hold; although I will tell you that each country's officers speak English with a different accent and sometimes the German must translate the French officer's English to the Polish officers.

I have made friends with the German chemical warfare soldiers, and they give me my fill of their strong coffee when I visit. We sometimes exchange our U.S. MREs (meals ready to eat) for their rations. Theirs are great—pâté, wurst, and something I haven't figured out yet. They love our meals, too. It is a great way to break up the monotony of the day.

20 SEP 2002

Not much went on today; however, this evening has been very exciting. I can't go into detail other than to say, as the Brits put it, "lots of drama." There is much air activity going on overhead at the moment. I will come back to this letter in a bit.

I also learned a couple of other terms from the Brits: "long drop" and "thunder box." That is what they call the outhouses. Such a sense of humor!

Sincerely,
Diggs

Hi Diggs –

Thanks for your interesting letter and beautiful photos from the Big A. Your teaching career is taking off, almost as successfully as your nightclub gig! You must be the most popular guy around. Keep working on the heating system! When you get into the native garb I hope you'll be able to send us pictures of yourself wearing the robes, turban, etc. Do they have harems out there, or is that just in Hollywood's version? I've been sharing your letters and photos with my parents and my sister, and we all send you our best wishes, our sincere thanks, and support and prayers. When I print your photos at work, my secretary gets a kick out of seeing them too. I appreciate your keeping in touch and keeping us civilians apprised of some of the inside poop on the situation over there. Thanks for being our ambassador and representing the best of the U.S. to the rest of the world. Keep safe, watch your back, take care my friend.

God bless,
Andrea

22 SEP 2002

I wound up teaching map reading to the Afghan officers once again. They love the maps and my style of teaching. I use my computer and a projector for my class. During the breaks I showed them a few American television commercials that are stored on my computer's hard drive. One was the Budweiser commercial "Wazzzz up?" It took a bit of explaining and translation for them to understand what the term meant. Now they all mimic the commercial. They think it is the funniest thing they ever heard. In actuality, I find it difficult not to roll on the floor laughing when I hear these guys screaming "Wazzzz up?" I think I'll have them work on a Denver Broncos cheer later.

I found out an interesting fact yesterday. I got my first "me-behind-the-wheel" driving experience on the Afghan roads. When I first arrived I thought there were just a ton of taxis in this country. As it turns out, the Taliban outlawed personal vehicles but allowed taxis. Everyone painted their cars to look like taxis and continued to drive! You now see new cars that aren't painted like cabs, but anything over one year old is yellow and white. Speaking of driving, you cannot get road rage here because everyone drives like hell. They even cut across the median into oncoming traffic to pass slower vehicles.

ABC was here today filming "A Day in the Life." It will air in October. I didn't get photographed—too busy teaching my class. You'll get an idea of some of the things we are doing here if you catch the program.

After a couple of trips to Bagram and some negotiation, I finally arranged for someone from the PX to come to us for a day in the near future. I'm now a hero on the compound. It's becoming commonplace for fellow soldiers to tell me that they are glad I am on the mission with them. I hope to keep everyone's spirits high. I will be putting out a weekly newspaper soon; anything to keep busy. It is my intent to move the Bombay Lounge into an abandoned building at our site. I'm offering boots as bribes to the Italian engineers in hopes that they will do most of the renovation to the building. The roof was blown off during a B-52 raid on this compound back when the Taliban occupied it.

Winter is setting in, and it is getting cold here now. In the mornings you can see your breath, and I'm not talking about just outside but in our rooms, also. Remember, we haven't any heat source. I'm actually sleeping in tee shirt, shorts, and socks now. I think a stocking cap may be in order. We are supposed to be getting heat soon, but I think it will probably show up around July—typical Army.

I've been following the news about the sniper in Virginia. Man, I'm glad I'm over here where it is safe!

Dearest Diggsy:

Can't tell you how much I enjoy reading your letters...it's like talking to you (only without the cocktail on the side). THANK YOU so much for the beautiful scarf! It was a lovely surprise and is just gorgeous. I am touched that you thought of me. It sure doesn't sound like an atmosphere very conducive to shopping. (My greatest fear here is that no one is watching my back when I pull out my American Express card! "LOOK OUT! Mass destruction of budget is imminent!")

I had intended to immediately write back to you after your last letter to see what else you might need that you might not ask for in a mass letter. Are there any kinds of food treats you miss that might travel well? Not sure what you can get at the PX, but I imagine there isn't much really exciting stuff. I do have an idea of one item that I'm going to send along. Also, I can burn CDs, if you're interested in any music. You know my general taste and collection—rattle off some artists that you and the gang might like, and I'll send you some tunes, if that's cool.

Loved reading about your creating "The Fabulous Bombay Lounge." Our Diggs...always the party facilitator. Sounds like a great idea, and I'm sure it's a much-needed taste of "normality" for all of you. If that's at all possible. Hey, a big warm, dry, dust-free bed and chilly martini aren't all they are cracked up to be....

Things here are always interesting in a normal sort of way! EDS is in the middle of a lot of layoffs. I managed to escape the one last week that greatly reduced our team. Was glad about that...it would be nice to keep my job through the holidays at least. But all is well...I'm glad to know you're doing well and have the opportunity to share your wonderful and zany personality with the locals and with the lucky troops (would that be the proper word?) serving with you. You have always been one of the best spirit-lifters I've ever known!

Let me know what you need, honey. I'd like to make you my "missionary" project! I'm thinking of and praying for you.... Take care of yourself.

Much love, many kisses and hugs...

Di

23 OCT 2002

Today I taught English along with Chaplain Andy at the Pol-e-charkhi school. The students are really moving along in their knowledge. The Afghan English teacher wants to participate in the class as a student, and he is constantly interrupting by shouting out the answers. He is a tiny man with a scraggly beard and bad teeth. He also has a high pitched voice that becomes even more shrill when he screams out the answer. It is obvious the students don't appreciate his participation, but none dare voice this. I might have a photo of me teaching to send with this e-mail. You'll have to note that I'm wearing my pistol, and the rifle is within easy reach.

I did get a huge compliment today from my interpreter. He told me that the Afghan officers thought I was their best teacher and were asking for me to teach more classes. This morning as I crossed the compound, I overheard two of the officers greeting each other with "Wazzz up?" What a hoot!

Don't let it be said that I'm not a merciful man. I'll end this letter now. I do appreciate all your kind thoughts, prayers, and concern. I will be just fine over here; the bad guys can't hit the broad side of a barn, so far.

Cheers!

I am teaching English to a boys' class at Pol-e-charkhi. Notice the deplorable conditions. No furniture, lights, heat, or adequate teaching tools are available.

31 OCT 2002

Dear Friends,

The evenings have turned cold. Our generators cannot carry the electric load we are consuming; hence, no coffee pots, no heaters (if we had any), computer use is limited, and no refrigeration—although everything is pretty much staying chilled now anyway, so what does that matter? We are allocating electricity for the water heaters, so every other day there is a lukewarm shower. I can really sympathize with the folks who grew up using an outhouse in the middle of winter.

The days here start out pretty nice. It reminds me of Colorado. In the early morning it is brisk with clear skies and no breeze. By noon we are at 70 degrees. The nights are clear, and as soon as the sun sets, it gets cold—I mean COLD. We are hitting the 30s at night. Every day is like camping out; run to the outhouse, and shave and shampoo with ice-cold water.

One of the problems we are running into now is that more mice are coming inside because of the cold. However, mice aren't the biggest problem; it is the cobras and scorpions that come in after the mice. One of the docs found a cobra curled up in his gear. If he had a constipation problem, that solved it. We are now very careful about what we leave on the ground and how we pick it up.

It's funny how some things never change; I remember hearing the stories from veterans of previous wars about powdered eggs and how awful they were. Nowadays the cooks use egg substitute out of a carton—appalling. I eat very little breakfast anymore. The highlight of my morning is the sporadic morning briefing at the German compound and having a cup of their coffee as time permits.

I've been assigned a bunch of additional responsibilities. Everyone at the embassy knows me by now, and I am referred to as Captain Diggs. One of my additional duties is to be the paymaster for the Afghan army. This is quite a headache; lots of driving around Kabul with a heavily armed escort, carrying enough cash for anyone in this country to retire for life. Eventually, I will be traveling to the outposts via military air to issue pay. This new duty has pulled me out of the field for the most part, but I still get out occasionally. I have to have some excitement to help the days pass.

Another hat I wear is coordinating VIP visits to our compound. The list of dignitaries that come through here would astound you. The mission we are running here is the most important one—rebuilding the Afghan army. Once a week, or so it seems, a VIP passes through. The typical visit will include an in-depth briefing, a tour, and a typical Afghan meal. Sometimes we include observation of training, if time and security permit it.

Among other things, I'm also the "social chairman" and coordinator between U.S. and ISAF forces. I had the Austrians, Italians, French, and Spanish over tonight for a traditional Afghan meal prepared by the cooks we hire to feed the Afghan army. This was a huge success. I consider it payback, since I have talked most of them into using their heavy equipment to fortify our compound. We will probably have these meals once a month now. The down side was that I broke my soda fast. I hadn't had a soda in two months, but there was nothing else to drink at the meal. I'll do better and bring my bottled water next time. I've been invited over to lunch with the Spanish this Sunday.

I got a tremendous response from you, my friends, in regard to school supply donations for the kids here. Once again the Americans have proved to be the most generous people in the world, without so much as a blink of the eye. We, the American soldiers, are also receiving boxes full of gifts from home. The Red Cross has been very good at distributing items that have been donated. Once a week, we get at least four large boxes of personal toiletries, candy, books, puzzles, snacks, envelopes, etc. It is like Christmas every week! I personally lack nothing. For those of you who have sent items, thanks! We also get stacks of mail from school kids and thank-you letters from adults. I wish there was time to write back to each and every one of them to thank them for their thoughtfulness.

We have an on-base Afghan barber who is paid a salary to cut the hair of the soldiers, and he charges one dollar for U.S. soldiers. He is actually better than most barbers I have used back home. He uses only shears and safety razors. Of course, he gives a splash of aftershave when he is finished. I had my hair cut very short today (as short as it has been in many years) and shaved off my mustache. I'm beginning to realize just how cold it gets without it. I think I'll let it grow out once again.

I've had several of you ask what I want to do when I get home. I've kicked around buying a house as soon as I know where I will be working for my bank. I may also buy a new Harley while here. There is a guy up at Bagram Air Base who will take your order here, the bike will be assembled in the States, and you pick it up at a predetermined location of your choice. We can get them at a very respectable discount. Taking into consideration what I sold mine for before coming here, for just a few more dollars I could have a brand new one. I'll have to give that some thought.

01 NOV 2002

Today was a day off. This morning we, the American military, challenged the French to a friendly game of soccer. I guess I should say the challenge was ours because they soundly beat us. Next week we will play American football. I expect a reversal in the outcome. After the game, which was held at the ISAF headquarters in downtown Kabul, we meandered over to the Italian section of the compound and had our fill of espresso. This was absolutely the most relaxed day I've had since coming here. There is great camaraderie between the different armies—after all, we have the military bond, and many of the countries represented here lost citizens in the 9/11 attacks.

The afternoon consisted of four of us driving through western Kabul in our Toyota pickup. It seemed that for miles we saw nothing but destroyed and uninhabitable housing areas. The people were absolutely thrilled to see us. The children yelled out, "How are you?" Everyone waved. The kids ran alongside the car waving and cheering. It really makes us feel like we are making a difference in their lives. I managed to sneak in a bit of shopping today. I think I was the hit around town; I wore jeans and a red Hawaiian shirt under my armor. Well, maybe not a hit, more like a target. I guess one must do something a bit zany once in awhile to keep life in perspective.

02 NOV 2002

Human bones are abundant here. Another skull has turned up, and it was placed on top of a World War II tank that sits just outside my front door. The doc said that the people in this region have very thin skulls, and after examining the skull I believe it must be true. The cranium on this skull is so thin. It had to be an Afghan skull because most of the teeth were missing or decayed, and it is smaller than an adult Russian, in my opinion. This is the first time I've actually sat down and examined a skull. Very interesting—I wonder who this was and what his life was like. When I first moved into my room, I found human ribs in the corner. The MPs that guard our west swear their post is haunted. Late at night they hear what they believe to be footsteps coming up the four flights of concrete stairs that lead to their post. I haven't been up to check it out yet, but will before I leave here.

03 NOV 2002

We had VIPs in today. I've been placed in charge of organizing and escorting their trips. This trip was a huge success. The VIPs are from the countries that have been donating supplies. There were two Pakistani officers in the bunch, and this caused quite a ruckus among the Afghanis. The Pakistanis supported the Taliban when they were in power, and their presence was not appreciated during this visit. The Afghanis did not voice this, but it was evident in their eyes.

The electricity shortage problem has been solved! As it turned out, the dryers were consuming too much electricity and shorting out the generators—not that the dryers worked anyway. Now everything is line dried. On the other hand, we can have coffee again! I'm using a coffee pot that my parents sent. Just waiting on some French coffee that Marcia, my sister who lives in France, had to send back to the States in order for it to get mailed here. That surely makes for an expensive cup of Joe!

Must run now.

Cheers!
Diggs

CHAPTER 6
TURNING 46 IN AFGHANISTAN

Diggs,

Greetings from your home church in Duncan, OK!! How are things going? Your Dad has passed on to me a copy of your latest news from big "A". I have enjoyed reading it and looking at the pictures he also brought by.

I'm interested in learning from you what our congregation might send to you to be shared with the children of Afghanistan. You mentioned some items for the kids in your class. We could sure gather some chalk and blackboard erasers, if that is what you could use a lot of. Think about it and let me know. It would be neat to know our kids were sending some things that would get in the hands of the Afghan children through you.

Your parents seem to be coping well with having their only son on foreign soil with the U.S. Armed Forces. I want to be supportive of them, and of you. Please know we are standing behind you and are proud of your service to our country. God bless and lead you!!

Tracy

Captain Brown,

My wife, Paula, and I got busy and rounded up a number of the items you requested. One package has educational posters and the other reference books, maps, chalk & erasers.

My view is that the real battle will be won by keeping the present conflict from becoming a "Clash of Civilizations". Of course overthrowing the Taliban and destroying Al-Qaeda's Terrorist Camps had to come first. Then the next phase will consist of providing security and stability, as you are doing now by teaching English and training a non-ethnic national Afghan Army. But in my view, the long term struggle will be won if we are successful in rebuilding a peaceful & stable Afghanistan. That is really where you come in by teaching English. Education will allow the Afghanis to eventually take control of their own lives and nation. So let me take this opportunity to tell you how much we appreciate the sacrifices you and people like you are making!

> *Sincerely,*
> *Ragan and Paula*

Hi!

I just finished your letter that was e-mailed and loved it! You are such a writer! You have a new future when you are all done in writing a book about your experiences. You could retire and spend your life at some remote tropical island, surrounded by beauty of all kinds!

Thanks for sharing with us. It does help us to understand what we are faced with, when you relay your experiences to us. And what a teacher! We all know here that you are great, now others are getting to experience that.

It is cold and white here. We had snow on Tues and again last night. It is really pretty and it appears that we have around 5 to 6 inches. I heard on the radio this morning that from Ft. Collins to Wyoming it was pretty bad. They had lots of snow and then a lot of fog this morning. Along with icy roads, it was pretty treacherous.

Take care and stay safe! We love you and want you home safe and sound!

> *Sending you our prayers*
> *for a safe return,*
> *Patty*

Dear Diggs,

The first thing in order is to wish you a very happy birthday and MANY, MANY MORE from your mom and dad. We are very

proud of you for many reasons. Take care and be alert. The second
thing is to vote today. Your mother and I have studied the ballot
very carefully and will vote our convictions. Many people have
had the opportunity to read your diary and were impressed. I
believe you will receive many benefits from this effort. Received
the package for Julie yesterday but did not have an opportunity
to deliver and today is a holiday for her in light of voting. Will
deliver tomorrow and you can bet your bottom dollar that you
made her day. Diggs, happy birthday from Mom and Dad. You
are always in our thoughts and prayers with all of our love. Just
thought of something— AS soon as you were born and Audrey
was out of recovery I went to the company car and got on the
radio announcing to the division of your arrival, sex, and name.
Everyone thought that was a great way to announce your arrival
and I received lot of kidding for many weeks.

> *Love,*
> *Mom and Dad*

05 NOV 2002

Happy birthday to me! I spent the day in the desert on patrol.
The rain came in unexpectedly, roaring over the mountains. The
day became very cold and damp in a hurry. The talcum-like sand
is so dry that it actually repelled the first few drops. The roads
became very slippery as the sand that did turn to mud was only
a quarter inch or so deep. I have never seen anything like this
before. The clouds reminded me of Colorado, hugging the
mountaintops. Funny, I had always assumed the tree in front of
my hooch had gray leaves. Well, now I know they are green—the
dust was washed off!

Speaking of birthday, I received many e-mails and a few gifts—
all of which I am thankful for. One of my banks sent a large
birthday cookie packed in a box of popped popcorn. This gift was
a huge success and was devoured within minutes by the troops.

The Afghanis say the rains stopped when the Taliban came to power. I'm glad to see rain now that we are here. These people really need some moisture. The roof over my bed collapsed from the downpour. It had a rocket hole that had been patched overhead, but I guess the precipitation loosened the cheap mortar enough to give way. I'm glad I wasn't under it when it came down. It was an interesting evening in my room being surrounded by old Russian helmets catching the water and sleeping on the only dry spot on the floor.

Ramadan started today and will run for a month. During daylight, the Muslims refrain from eating, drinking, sex, and simple pleasures like smelling flowers—anything basically that can be enjoyable. They do a lot of praying during this time. We will be cutting back their workdays to half. As part of their ritual, they will dine at 0330 and 1900 (that's 3:30 a.m. and 7:00 p.m.) in order to avoid eating during daylight. In honor of the new government, for the first time in over 10 years, the night curfew will be lifted. It is expected that this will be a permanent change.

06 NOV 2002

I got the best birthday present I could have ever asked for...the Republicans took control of Congress! I'll bet Iraq backs down now; if not, to hell with them and here we go!

I spent most of the day laying plastic over the new hole in the roof. This was quite an undertaking. I really don't like standing on a rooftop near a busy road. I managed to use sandbags, wood, and plastic to rig a patch. I also recovered some discarded tin cans and fashioned them into a rainspout. With a little luck, the next time it rains I will stay reasonably dry.

It rained again tonight, and low and behold I stayed dry! I'm going to move my belongings back into my room tomorrow. We are finished with the rain for the next few days, according to our Air Force weathermen—and they are rarely wrong, unlike the weathermen you see on the television.

07 NOV 2002

The bad guys have stepped up their activities. When the Afghan winter sets in, the majority of the passes between Pakistan and Afghanistan will be closed. They feel they must show the populace that the Americans are too weak to defend them, so they attack villages, set off car bombs, and fire rockets at our compounds. The Taliban fear that over the long winter, the people will forget the lessons they are giving them now. Not much is happening around us, but more to the east and south.

We received a shipment of Russian jeeps called Uaz. They are junk, and a number of them are dead-lined at the moment. Some of the Afghanis spat at our new vehicles when we drove through town. I'm guessing it is because they were reminded of the Russians and didn't realize that Americans are driving them now. We think we've solved this problem by painting Afghan flags on the doors. Indeed, there is now a positive reaction from the townsfolk.

Rockets! Got to go!

09 NOV 2002

It warmed up this morning for a bit, but turned cold and dreary again this afternoon. I slept extremely well last night due to the fact that I broke down yesterday and bought a blanket made out of 60 fox pelts. I hope none of you are PETA (People for the Ethical Treatment of Animals). Well, I hope it is fox and not Fido. I have this hang-up about clinging to the last bit of civilization I can— and sleeping under sheets is it. I've been refusing to sleep in a sleeping bag and had been sleeping under a wool blanket I bought at the bazaar. The new blanket is a dream. It does have that doggie smell, but not bad. I also bought a couple of mink hats in the Russian style.

Many of you know what an animal lover I am. I am missing my two birds back home. I am going to try and buy a canary later if I can find one. I've seen them around town at storefronts.

They are real singers. I got to play with a bomb-sniffing dog today at the embassy. What a great dog, Belgium something-or-other, well-mannered with a good temperament. I would love to get a dog when I return home.

When you think of morale you can generally go two directions—good or bad. It is a funny thing, just when you think things are so bad you can't stand it anymore, someone cracks a joke about the conditions and everything is fine. You have to have a sense of humor! Speaking of which, we should have our water running again within the next 24 hours. ☺

10 NOV 2002

Ah, a shower, and hot to boot! Got a load of laundry done and, of course, had to let it hang on the line to dry. I do have this figured out to a degree—I just give my clothes a good shake when I remove them from the line and most of the caked dust falls off.

More rockets today. When rockets come in they make a swooshing sound that varies in duration. If it is a miss, the swoosh is long as they pass overhead. When the impact is going to be nearby, the swoosh is short in duration followed by a thundering bang! There is nothing we can do about the near hits except dust ourselves off and look to see if we have any new holes in our uniforms.

The battalion of French soldiers who occupy the corner of our compound is shipping out this Friday. They are a great group of guys. Tonight they had a private party for the guys leaving and their American guests. I was invited and had the opportunity to drink some wonderful champagne from a bottle that had been opened with a sword. There was a lot of singing and camaraderie.

I am sad to see them go, but happy for them that they are. I hope their replacements are of the same caliber. One of the French majors gave me a commemorative medal. We gave them a plaque and certificates of appreciation in return.

The outgoing battalion commander and his bodyguard have a tradition they keep at every party. (The bodyguard is a huge East Islander of some type—probably Tahitian.) The commander and guard both climb up on a large table, and as everyone sings, they jump up and down on the table to the beat of the singing until the table collapses. Everyone cheers them on until the grand finale, followed by a thunderous round of applause.

Soldiers (or "Joes," as we say) are the same no matter where you go. It is a brotherhood.

Well, I guess five pages are enough for now. I will try and get another letter out before Thanksgiving.

Warm regards,
Diggs

CHAPTER 7
GROUNDHOG DAY

Hey Diggs!

You sure know how to treat your Godson right. He was so excited about his camel. He has played "army" with it everyday. He took it to Show-N-Tell last Friday where all the kids thought it was pretty cool to be handmade and from the big "A". This morning he was so cute. I told him to make sure he ate all his eggs "protein" so he would grow up to be big and tall like his dad. In all sincerity he looked up at me and said, "But I want to grow up and be just like Uncle Diggs Mom."

The kids in his class indicated they would like to collect some things for your school like paper, pencils, crayons, etc. if those are things you think you need. They can draw and send pictures too. As Max told me, "I understand how hard it is to start school. It's taken me a long time to get to where I am today!" (3½ months of school so far). Let me know what you think and what items might help. I gather we would send these things to your "regular" address?

Anyway, met your dream trustfund girl. She backpacks throughout the country, is a real sports enthusiast and cute. She was featured in an article for a fitness magazine recently too.

Take Care and Much Love,
Lolly and the Gang

Diggs!

You have absolutely no idea how happy I am to get your e-mail! Tomorrow is Veteran's Day, and I plan on reading your information on the big "A", and showing the pictures. I just stared at them in almost disbelief. Wow. It is going to bring more of a mental image to the kids' minds. We've heard about the walls that are painted black for a chalk board, now they get to see it.

They love to talk about what's going on over there, and learn as much as they can about the situation. I am so lucky to have such a great class this year!

We are working on a class project right now to get some school supplies to send over to the schools over there. We've got so much stuff already. The kids have taken it upon themselves to visit all the office supply stores and Targets and stuff to get donations. We are just trying to figure out how we are going to get it there now. We have about 20 really big boxes.

I can't believe it is going to get that cold there. Yowza! That is extreme weather change! Do you have any type of heat there? Sorry if that's a silly question.

That is great that the local people are so welcoming of you guys. I can't imagine their world and all that they've been through. I wonder how they know who to trust and believe anymore. People keep saying just bomb the hell out of Afghanistan, but it is important to remember those poor people there who are just trying to survive and make a better life for themselves. God we are so lucky to live in America!!!

I wanted to ask you about something... we received a little woven rug thing from a soldier over there that he got from a street vendor. It has the World Trade Centers on it, both on fire and a small plane flying over. It also has U.S.A. on it, and September 11. But the thing on it that is concerning is the American Flag... it is upside down. When I first got it, I didn't show the kids because I didn't know what to make of it. Could it be a mistake? Is this how they are taught the flag is, or did they truly mean to disrespect us? I'll take a digital picture of it tomorrow at school and e-mail it to you so you can see it.

I will send some pictures to you tomorrow of the class....we've taken a bunch of digital pix at school. I am glad you are writing Ally and Logan. Ally is a very sweet girl and your letter put her on a high. You've really captured Logan's interest in the whole situation. He has been so engaged in the class discussions lately. Thanks!

I hope you get a moment to just relax today. Thank you so much for writing and saying what you say. Hearing it from a true American Hero makes these kids sit up and listen. It will be great to have you home in Colorado again, and hopefully a visit to Parker!

Ciao,
Michelle

12 NOV 2002

Dear Friends and Family,

There is so much going on here that I wish I could tell you, but unfortunately I cannot. I will tell you that we are winning the war, but it is going to be a long haul.

I spend long hours fulfilling my daily duties, and at times it seems like I do not have enough hours to get everything done that I wish. I was thinking about it yesterday, and if things go as they were originally planned, I only have 240 more days here. A better way to look at it is only 32 more Thursday night movies!

Our days all seem to roll into one. There is a movie called "Groundhog Day," starring Bill Murray. It is about a man who lives each day over and over again until he gets everything right. I'm living it, so it seems. We have Fridays off, as that is the Islamic holy day. This odd day off throws my habitual day pattern off a bit. Saturday always seems like Monday. I'm now using a notepad for a to do list, something that I never had to do before.

Again, I want to thank all of you who have sent items for me and school supplies for the students. We will deliver the supplies in a couple of months or so. There is still one large shipment from a school in Colorado that will be coming in soon. At this point I'm going to have to ask that you send no more donations. We have run out of storage space and cannot hand out the supplies until school resumes at full capacity.

Another project we are working on (with winter setting in) is winterizing the school so that in the future it may be used

67

year-round. We placed plastic where the glass once was, but this isn't enough insulation. We've taken up donations here on our base and will spend the money to refurbish one room. Hopefully, as time moves on we will get the rest of the rooms finished. They must be patched and painted and equipped with blackboards, furniture, and most of all, heaters.

I don't know how much longer I will be able to teach, as my work load has become very intense. Chaplain Andy will continue, no doubt, because his days are free. There is a winter break at the moment, so school activities have come to an end. I don't know if I mentioned this or not in previous letters, but the Taliban burned down a couple of schools in our vicinity. They are so against Western influence and education of the children.

I am amazed how many soldiers are attending church service here. We built a small chapel and hold three services every Sunday, plus a Bible study every Wednesday. I am usually working every day, all day, and many times into the night, so I haven't been to service as I should; although the chaplain and I talk on a regular basis. He gets a big kick out of helping with the Thursday night movies. When I first heard that a chaplain was going to deploy with us, I had my doubts; however, Chaplain Andy has proven to be a valuable asset and a good friend. He has done much to bolster the morale here and keep the spiritual compass pointing true north.

As Thanksgiving approaches, I have had many thoughts lately about what we, as Americans, should be thankful for. The list is too long to go through, and I can't preach to the choir. I know there are plenty of you who understand the sacrifices the "Greatest Generation" made, along with the others who have gone before us. I just have a feeling there is a generation of younger adults who might not fully appreciate what they have and cannot comprehend ever being without. Maybe September 11th was the eye-opener that our country needed, but it is a shame it happened at the price of so many innocent lives. We did recently receive a pile of letters from high school sophomores that were supportive—nice to see that it is not just grade school children writing. It is reassuring.

I hope that this Thanksgiving everyone will take a serious moment and really think about all we have to be grateful for.

14 NOV 2002

We graduated another battalion of Afghan National Army today. The ceremony was long and tedious, but it was impressive to see the soldiers passing in review. Their cadre from the previous army of a decade ago was taught to march by the Russians in the goosestep fashion. We decided not to try and change that; there are more important matters on which to train. Just before the ceremony, one of the small children who regularly attends these types of ceremonies was marching across the parade field. He couldn't have been more than four years old. As he marched up to the battalion, all the soldiers gave him a round of applause and encouragement. I've included a photo.

The young Afghan boy goosesteps, much to the delight of the soon-to-be graduated battalion of soldiers.

A contingent of cheerleaders from the Washington Redskins and Wizards are going to be up at Bagram Air Base. I arranged for 12 selected soldiers to take the day to visit Bagram and see the show. They were thrilled to death. As you may or may not know, we don't get USO-type shows at our location due to the perception of a high threat level.

I've been working on the Australian who is in charge of morale events to get something here, but it is going to take time. His name is Stuart and he is one hilarious guy. He reminds me of the "Croc Hunter." He is a major in the Australian army. His family consists of a wife and two children who dearly miss their daddy. He is really into snow skiing, so I've invited them to Colorado to challenge our slopes when this is all over.

The boys we sent to watch the cheerleader show made it home tonight late and told me that they had the best time. We sent a couple of the German soldiers along, and they couldn't thank me enough. I've now been invited to the German compound for a barbecue dinner. I've also arranged a shooting event with the Germans so that we can become familiar with each other's weapons systems. We will be shooting next week. I will give up my slot in this shooting event to allow one of the enlisted guys to shoot and receive a German commemoration medal.

That's all for now. It is late and I will be up early.

Sincerely,
Diggs

CHAPTER 8
CIVILIZATION AT LAST!

Happy Monday!

I read your information about Afghanistan to the kids today. You could hear a pin drop in here as they were listening. These kids come from a very comfortable background, and I don't think they realized such conditions could even exist. I printed out the pictures you sent to show them, too. What a statement they made.

I hadn't read your letter before telling you about our school supply drive we are doing. I think it is great that you want to do the same thing. We have lots of supplies already, and should be getting more. Do you have any ideas on how we could get it there? I used to know a bunch of big wigs at Buckley that I thought could help us out, but they are all gone. I thought maybe we could send it through the military to save on cost of shipping. And should we send it to your unit attention you? Are there any requirements as far as what we can send and how we can send it?

The kids are also putting together a holiday package for your unit. Are there certain things (besides alcohol) that you aren't permitted to have? Can we send pop? Magazines? Disposable cameras? A furnace? oh, sorry...

Thanks for explaining to the kids that the rug makers most likely did not know that the American flag was upside down or right side up when they wove the rug. I wondered how much the people there actually know about Sept 11, I mean what REALLY happened. Do they have a daily paper there? Is it censored? Again, I don't know how those people know who to trust and who not to trust.

Our class is getting ready to go to Outdoor Ed. We go up to Estes Park for 3 days and hike all day and learn about rocks, minerals, and plate tectonics. We get to stay in cabins. I am hoping it isn't below freezing while we're up there. They just got 2 feet of snow. Snow I can handle, cold toes and nose I can't. Yes, I am a wimp!

Do you get updates on all that's happening with Iraq and stuff? Do you get CNN or MSNBC? I'd die without the news channels. I'm addicted to news. Sometimes I worry about myself!

Well, I've got to run and teach math class. I am so glad you have e-mail... much easier than waiting 3 weeks for a letter. I am sure you get tons of e-mail sent your way, so thanks so much for replying to mine.

Let me know about the school supplies. Together we can make this project happen. I am so excited!!!

Just so you know, we are a year-round school, and we go "off track" November 27th and don't come back till January 5th (or somewhere around there). I will still be able to e-mail you of course, but the kids will be gone. I'd like to get these supplies sent off before they go on break.

Thanks for freezing your butt off for us back here in the U.S. Thanks for eating sand with each meal. Thanks for making a difference. You are amazing!

Ciao~
Michelle

15 NOV 2002

I was finally able to get someone from the PX down to our location for a couple of days. In the past, the only way we could get to the PX was an hour-long dangerous convoy to Bagram Air Force base. The PX isn't at all like it used to be in the old days. A few years ago, it was decided that the government wouldn't subsidize the prices the way they used to. We now pay the same or a bit more than you do at Wal-Mart, and the only advantage is no tax. The disadvantage is lack of selection, but at least we have something to select!

We drove up to Bagram Friday morning to pick up the PX folks. We eventually loaded up two trucks of merchandise to bring back to Kabul. Four PX employees rode down with us. They are civilians, many with prior military service. They wear Army pattern uniforms and body armor when traveling with us. The lady who is in charge of the PX at Bagram has been here 15 months! She volunteered for the duty and her husband is okay with it. I think they get excellent pay and benefits for being here—they must.

The PX staff we brought down is a great mix. There is Paula, the head honcho; she is probably in her mid-40s and just a sweetheart. Rick is former Army, but now a Harley kind of guy. He has an earring, scraggly beard, smokes like a chimney, and has a great personality. Tony is a young man of Hispanic background. He is polite and very quiet. Grahame is from Scotland and is one funny guy. I have a hard time with his accent as he is from Glasgow and uses a lot of Scottish slang. Grahame sells the Harley Davidsons and an assortment of American built automobiles.

On this particularly dirty day, I rode shotgun on top of the Hummer. Of course it is a long, hot, and dusty ride. By the time we got back to our base, I looked like a raccoon with white around my eyes where my sunglasses blocked the dirt.

I've mentioned in previous letters the high and dramatic mountains here. They are now peaked with snow and are just beautiful. It makes me homesick for Colorado. I did go through that homesick stage a couple of weeks ago when the birthday cards came in, but am over it now. Anyway, the snow is creeping farther down the mountains every day. Soon we will have snow on the ground here.

The PX was able to set up in one of our bombed-out buildings and do two hours of business with the U.S. soldiers and French soldiers on our base. We had to shut down the store at dusk because there are no lights in this building. Everyone was thrilled that they were here. We had crab legs for dinner in our mess hall. By the way, the Army, in its infinite wisdom and political correctness, now calls the mess halls dining facilities. The PX employees were as thrilled about the crab legs as we all were. We usually have a decent meal once a week; it is good for morale.

This afternoon, Major Bruce and I grabbed an interpreter and walked a few miles to a village just south of us. The children, as well as the adults, were curious about us, but once they saw the camera they became quite the hams. It was nice to be able to show them the digital picture immediately after taking it with the LCD display. As I have mentioned before, the Taliban outlawed photographs, so these kids have never seen a photo of themselves. I got a couple of great shots. My favorite is a man looking over a wall. As we were taking pictures of his house, he began yelling at us. At first I thought he was angry, but the interpreter told us he wanted us to take his picture. I did. He climbed over the wall to see the photo on the camera's digital display, and he was as happy as could be. He invited us to dinner at his home, but we had to get back to our base camp before dark. At least that is a good excuse. I've mentioned before that if we eat on the economy here, chances are we will get deathly ill.

One of my favorite interpreters is Mahboobla. I call him "Boobs," and he gets a kick out of it. He is a good kid, 26 years old, and getting married in three weeks. All of our interpreters are good, and they can make a difference in what we are trying to achieve. They all want to come to America, and who doesn't? Wish we could get them to the States; they are very dedicated and loyal. A good interpreter here makes $700 a month, which is a small fortune, but I feel inflation is going to be rampant as foreign governments continue to pour money into this country.

16 NOV 2002

We opened the PX today at 10:00 a.m. The ISAF (International Security Assistance Force) was invited over, and we had a steady parade of Europeans here. The PX was full all day.

At the end of the six-hour shift the PX had sold a total of $12,000 in merchandise, not counting nine Harley Davidson motorcycles and four cars that can only be purchased by American soldiers. I bought a Harley Electra Glide at a great price—just $2,000 more than what I sold my old motorcycle for (sorry, Mom). The cars and motorcycles are direct from the factory, so we get super prices. They will be shipped to our home of record by the time we return.

There was a riot today at the university in Kabul. Four students were shot and killed by police. There are students who are reported to be Taliban stirring things up. They are armed and have even tried to dress like Americans and cause problems on the campus. I would be interested to see these guys dressed as they think Americans would dress. How about that accent? I think I have mentioned before that the Taliban are not the brightest people on the planet. They are, however, ruthless.

Tonight I took our PX guests to the Italian compound for the grand opening of the "Pizza Oven." The Italians are an engineering unit, and in their spare time have put great effort into building an authentic Italian pizzeria. It is beautiful—just as you would see in Italy. Of course, you have to take into consideration that they do not have the very nice fixtures that they would at home, but what they don't have, they have fabricated to the best of their ability.

The Italian ambassador was there, along with the Cardinal of Kabul. The place was really packed, even though it was an *invitation only* event. They had wine, pizza (of course), assorted meats, rice, and cheese. I was in heaven, as were the PX people; just the icing on the cake to get them back down here for the months to come.

After the Italian compound, I took them to the Spanish compound to watch flamenco dancing. A couple of days ago I gave a Holyoke, Colorado, baseball cap to a Spanish major. When we showed up, he greeted us proudly wearing the cap. We spent just a short time at this location before calling it a night.

Needless to say, the PX employees have decided that they should come down once a month and run a store out of our compound. This will be a huge morale boost!

Things are moving along here. I'm thankful for your prayers.

Sincerely,

Diggs

CHAPTER 9
THANKSGIVING / WHERE'S THE HEAT?

Dear Diggs,

We are anxiously awaiting your return. Things just aren't the same without you here. Your sense of humor, confidence, and friendliness are missed more and more daily. It seems like there isn't a day that goes by that someone does not mention your name. This is my first investment campaign that you haven't been here for and the effects are felt; long story!

I could say thank you a million times and it would not be able to come close to expressing the gratitude I feel for the job you are doing. You are the reason we have the freedoms we have. You are the reason why we can walk safely through our streets. You are the reason we can live our lives without fear of military invasion. It takes a person of integrity and greatness to put millions of people's lives ahead of his own. How you do this amazes me. For these reasons, I am forever in debt to you. I feel protected knowing there is someone like you over there fighting for our safety and peace of mind. You will always be in my thoughts and prayers.

Love,
Christine

17 NOV 2002

Dear Family and Friends,

We were getting excited about Brown and Root coming to our compound to install heaters. Then the bad news came that the heaters aren't even in the country and aren't expected anytime soon. We are now expecting the heaters sometime around mid-Decemburrrrrrrrrrr. I've been using propane and a heating element I bought off the local economy to heat my area. It doesn't make things much warmer but does knock out the chill. I've left it on all night, every night, so the guys who share my area will be a bit more comfortable. Ran out of fuel today and didn't have the chance to buy more. Tonight is going to be a cold one! Don LaRue sent me a Pendleton blanket from Arizona and it certainly has made a difference.

I've been receiving letters from a couple of children in Colorado. I wrote to them after getting one of the "For Any Soldier" letters. Great kids; so intelligent. Their teacher has written a couple of times, also. I plan on visiting their class when I get home and let them meet the person they've been writing. I once wrote to a soldier in Vietnam, but never got a return. A lot of children have sent out letters, but there isn't enough time to respond to all of them. The letters are excellent reading. The kids are so innocent and sweet.

I have great news! The Aussie has e-mailed me to let me know that the USO representative wants to come down this week to meet me and discuss getting some entertainment here! Wow! I can't tell you how much that will be appreciated. I have been looking into getting the Denver Bronco cheerleaders here but have been meeting resistance from their owner. Anyone out there have any pull? After all, most of us are from Colorado and are definitely Bronco fans.

We have MPs here from Massachusetts, and they are New England Patriots fans, of course. We bet them on the Bronco/ Patriots game; loser serves chow for a day. Well, Denver won and we made orange hats for the MPs to wear while they served the meals. It was really funny and they were good sports.

I have to admire the MPs; they are running 12-hour shifts and practically living on top of each other in one of the smaller buildings. They have good morale, great attitude, and are professional. Most of them are kids—well, I guess that is relative to my age. I don't know what we would do without them. They have my respect, and their commander is one sharp soldier.

21 NOV 2002

Because the heaters won't be in until mid-December, I've decreased my showers to two a week. We have warm water, but the walk to and from the shower point in the cold is just too much. Sometimes the pipes freeze, also.

We've moved one of our Afghan army battalions to a new location off post, and we've taken another one on a combat run. They are good soldiers. Funny story about these people, but maybe a bit much for some of you. SO, IF YOU ARE SQUEAMISH, DON'T READ THE NEXT PARAGRAPH.

In this country there very few toilets as we know them at home. The typical toilet is a hole in the ground that you straddle. Often, any spot outdoors is good for doing the business, and that is evident. We bought portable toilets for our Afghanis. The next thing we knew they looked like Smurfs! They were washing in them! After we explained what they were for, they began to use them; however, instead of sitting down, they tried to stand on them and straddle the hole. What a mess! Then, when we moved them to their new compound that had the hole in the ground toilets (something *we* don't even have), they used rocks to wipe themselves and clogged up the holes! It was suggested that we give them classes. This is one class that I am not going to instruct!

OKAY, YOU CAN READ AGAIN.

Something that makes me very proud of the men we are training is the fact that when payday comes, some are refusing to take their pay. They say they are here for the country! We have to talk these guys into taking the money, and although I'm sure part of it is for show, it makes me proud to be working with them. There is hope for the new Afghan army!

One of the things we are noticing now that it is cold is the large number of children who are out scrounging for fuel to burn for warmth. It is amazing how diligent they are, using this tool that resembles a short hoe and digging up a scrub that is very thorny and about the size of a softball. They will spend the day doing this and filling gunnysacks. As sparse as the vegetation is here, they manage to pick up these thorn plants barehanded and fill a couple of sacks in a day!

Another thing about the kids out in the countryside is that they will run great distances barefoot over rocky terrain when they see one of our vehicles. When I say great distances, I mean it. I've seen them come at a dead run from a half a mile away. They want to wave and yell, "How are you?" They expect candy, which I don't give out often. I don't believe in teaching them how to be beggars.

Here is some great news! My roommates and I bought a small stove in town for $20 and spent the day installing it and winterizing our room. The stove is a beautifully hand-tooled tin piece. It is about the size of a 30-gallon barrel, and the craftsmanship is exquisite. This stove has brought my morale up to a new high! I think it is more psychological than anything else. The stove only keeps a small area of the room warm, and we huddle around it just before lights out. My corner still has a cold breeze coming through it at night.

22 NOV 2002

The water is out again. It will be four days before we have any, if we are lucky.

26 NOV 2002

I've decorated the bush in front of my hooch with Christmas lights and decorations that were sent from home. The tank next to it has also been lit, along with the Bombay Lounge sign. On Thursday after Thanksgiving dinner, I plan on having a Christmas tree lighting ceremony. We will have hot instant cider that we have saved from the care packages, and the chaplain will say a few words. Then it is off to movie night, featuring the Clint Eastwood war movie "Kelly's Heroes." I expect a big crowd at both events; the guys are looking for a break in the action.

LATER

We had a great deal of "drama" late tonight. Several rockets streaked across our perimeter (narrowly missing our taller buildings) and crashed into the soccer field a block or so away. Their thunderous blasts broke out some of the few remaining windows in our compound. I guess that it is good every once in awhile to have some excitement, as long as no one is hurt. These incidents remind us to stay diligent at all times.

27 NOV 2002

I will be out for a few days and will get back to you later. Have a great Thanksgiving.

Regards!

Diggs

CHAPTER 10
THE CHEERFUL MAN

Hi Diggs,

Thank you for your Thanksgiving greetings and informative e-mails. Your prose is poignant, pithy, positive, and humorous. You are better than Norman Vincent Peale (but not quite up to Emma Peel yet ;-). I and my family appreciate your keeping us in the loop on what you and your soldiers are encountering and overcoming over there. We watched the ABC Thanksgiving night program and saw your base KMTC. Thanks for letting us know about it.

Just wanted to say that at Thanksgiving this year, I am thankful for you and our Armed Forces who selflessly and courageously are defending our freedom and making the world a better place—not only for us but for all those persons whose lives you touch and who benefit by your being there doing your job for God and Country. I'm proud to know you, my friend. You're a good man, and an inspiration and uplifting spirit to us all. You are in my prayers and thoughts everyday as you brave the winter and intrinsic dangers on the other side of the planet. Sending you warmest wishes for the holiday season and always.

Take care.
Andrea

01 DEC 2002

Dear Friends and Family,

One of the things that Army Special Forces is renowned for is "winning the hearts and minds" of the populace in the region of conflict. We do this in several ways. When we train with the soldiers we eat their food, use their weapons, and treat them as equals. We treat the people here with respect, careful not to offend their religious mores, and we learn their culture. Another way is to use our medical team and veterinarians to perform MEDCAPs (Medical Civil Assistance Program or Medical Capabilities Mission). Basically, they will go to a remote village for two or three days and see everyone who is willing to come forward with an ailment. In these poor countries, MEDCAPs are immensely popular. No one passes up the chance to take care of their children or themselves. We've had several MEDCAPs since our arrival, and they have all been received well. The Taliban doesn't want the MEDCAPs to take place, and in the past they have attacked the villages where these missions of mercy are occurring.

I know I've mentioned in previous letters the poor state of health the people have here, especially with their eyes. It is not uncommon to see an individual with one blind eye or an eye missing. We have with us one of the nation's top pediatric eye surgeons as one of our doctors. A few weeks ago one of our soldiers noticed a rug merchant's son with one crossed eye. The boy couldn't be more than four years old. Major John and I sought out the child last week and found him at his father's shop on Chicken Street. We brought the boy to our camp and had the surgeon look him over. As it turns out, the surgeon says he can repair the eye, and we will have the surgery scheduled for next week at no expense to the family. The father wanted to give us rugs in exchange for the service, or in gratitude, but we politely declined. Another heart and mind won—and one win will lead to others.

One of the remarkable things to me is that many of the children now know who I am and flock to me. I make it a point to deal with the children in the market by haggling with them over the prices of their merchandise instead of dealing with their parents. Of course, I always let them win, at a fair price. Many don't know my name but call me the "cheerful man." I don't know how to take that; some of the guys here are called "the lion" or "the storm," but I'm the "cheerful man." How do you think that goes over with a bunch of Green Berets?

Here is another project for those wishing to make donations—we could use more toothbrushes and small tubes of toothpaste. I guess it goes without saying that dentists here are as rare as hen's teeth, no pun intended. The typical citizen dunks a finger in water and uses it as a toothbrush. I could hand these out all day long if anyone is interested in sending them.

I've noticed that I don't flinch anymore when there is an explosion. Some of the guys still do, and I am amazed because we hear so many explosions of different natures. The swooshing noise made by the rockets when they pass overhead tends get my attention, but as I have stated before, the bad guys are lousy shots.

I've also mentioned the mice that come into our rooms to stay warm. I found a hamster under my mattress a few days ago. Hamsters apparently are native to this region, but they aren't brown like the ones I used to have as a child; instead they are gray. I caught him and to my surprise he was pretty docile. I didn't have the heart to put him out in the cold, so I let him go. I have been putting food out for him every night and he has been cleaning it up. If I had some sort of cage I would catch him, but I don't. Besides, he doesn't poop in my quarters—as far as I know.

01 DEC 2002

After nights of having guys come and hang out in our room just to experience the limited heat, the idea of buying tin stoves on the local market has caught on with everyone in our camp. The supply section went so far as to order a truck full of chopped wood for the base. What a difference just a bit of heat can make. We still have to wear coats in our rooms, but no gloves or stocking caps. Unfortunately, my corner of the room is still as cold as a crypt.

In our headquarters building, we still don't have heat, and at times it is so difficult to use the computers due to the cold. Using gloves is out of the question. It is actually warmer outside than

...the building. We have received the initial supply of heaters from Brown and Root. We will place this first shipment in the billets of our Afghan trainees. It is more important to keep them warm at the moment. We are being told that we will see our heaters within three weeks.

You've heard the saying, *Desperation* is the mother of invention. Naw, I know it is actually *necessity*, but desperation seems more appropriate at the moment. I made another modification to my bed by adding a canopy to catch my body heat, or at least block the breeze. The canopy is just a couple of feet above me and seems to help. My room is starting to look like a Bedouin tent with the rugs hanging on the wall to block the breeze that finds its way though the rocket damaged walls.

I can't complain too much about the cold. This morning I saw three children—probably ranging in age from three to six— huddled around a tiny fire by the road. Scenes like this break my heart. Some of these kids are barefoot or wearing sandals and wrapped in thin wool blankets. They don't have much for protection, but that is true for most people I have seen. They are a hardy bunch who are used to a life without many creature comforts, not by choice.

I guess it did get colder than I thought last night; the water bottles in my room froze solid.

02 DEC 2002

Today I went to Bagram Air Force Base and filmed a short tape for FOX TV. It was one of those "Hi, Mom" spots. It should air internationally over the next three weeks or so, but I don't know the times or dates. I could only use Captain Bob Diggs in my spot. No last name could be used due to the threat against Special Forces soldiers' families by al Qaeda. My last name on my uniform was covered with tape. I'll be interested to see if any of you view this. Let me know if you see it.

I was also interviewed a few days ago by the *Houston Chronicle* concerning the "hearts and minds" aspect of warfare and the English teaching that Chaplain Andy and I do at the local school. I'm not sure when that story will be out, but today they asked for photos of one of the classes.

03 DEC 2002

Last night we had a tremendous windstorm that really kicked up the dust. There was very little ambient light because the moon was in the final quarter, and the dust appeared almost as a haze due to its fineness. I expected to see snow on the ground this morning, but did not. It turned out to be a beautiful day—just a bit cool. As the day wore on the temperature dropped, and it is once again a bitter, freezing cold. I did get one reprieve today— I received a package of flannel sheets from Lanna. THANK YOU!

Harley Davidson e-mailed me and said the Electra Glide I ordered for delivery when I get home isn't available anymore, so I stepped up to a Road King Classic. It is a much nicer bike and will hold a higher value longer. When I finally get home I plan on taking a two-week trip on it to visit friends and family. A guy can dream, can't he?

04 DEC 2002

I have received several boxes of school supplies today and a couple of e-mails from children back home promising to send more. One elementary school sent me their school's tee shirt with an American flag on the front. Beth Clarken has started a campaign at Community First Bank, my old bank of employment, to gather school supply donations. I am overwhelmed by the generosity of the American people. Many of you have sent cards, toiletries, cigars, foodstuff, and school supplies. Thank you, thank you, and thank you. Do me a favor and when the war kicks off in Iraq, show that same spirit and generosity for the guys who will be in the big battle.

One thing I have noticed—and it is a bit overwhelming—is the fact that wherever we go people of all ages give us the "thumbs-up" and shout out, "Thank you!" I mean everywhere! This is so remarkable. I know I can't even imagine what these people have been through in the past 30 years. Some of them have known nothing but constant war, and now here we are as liberators. Our war on terror is having a tremendous impact on their lives, more than you can imagine. This is how terrorists will be defeated—when people the world over recognize that we are a giving country that can help them better themselves and experience their first true taste of freedom.

I made a wooden sign to hang in our new mortar pit. It is a tradition in the military to name roads, buildings, and other structures for your fallen comrades. When we first got here, there was a dog on our base that had been raised from a puppy by the previous unit. "Porkchop" was a large mixed-breed of some sort and just the friendliest dog you could meet. She got hit by a vehicle a month or so ago. The mortar pit's sign is in the shape of a dog's head and has "Porkchop Pit" painted on it. The new name makes for interesting radio traffic to and from the gunners.

06 DEC 2002

Today Ramadan ended. I gathered up the excess long johns, gloves, stocking caps, and tee shirts I had brought along and gave them to a few of the Afghan soldiers as a gift. They were thrilled to receive what I gave. I also threw in some candy bars and canned tuna. Some of these troops have never had fish before! What a treat for them.

We are expecting attacks for the next couple of days with the end of Ramadan. The Taliban and al Qaeda have put out a $10,000 reward for killing Americans. I don't think many people are interested in the offer, but you never know. The reward is more than some of these people will make in a lifetime. We are going to be exceptionally careful for the remainder of the week.

We just finished filming a television greeting for ABC's "Good Morning America." My unit wanted me to be the spokesperson for the group shot, and I also did a single for myself. I wore a Santa hat with my uniform for the filming. If you see the spot, note that everyone's nametag on their uniform is covered. We had a good time with the TV crew and got a morale boost out of it. It is always good to see an unfamiliar face from back home.

I'm wondering how low morale will sink as we near Christmas. I'm doing everything I can imagine to keep spirits high. Diana Sinea sent me some festive foodstuffs, so I will hold a soirée for some of the guys on Christmas Eve.

One of the other captains here wants to write a screenplay along with me. I have a great story line. If anyone of you knows a genuine writer out there, I'd be interested in collaborating with him or her.

Must run now. Thanks for all the support!

Cheers!
Diggs

CHAPTER 11
TRAGIC TIMES

Dear Diggs,

You just remember with God's armor nothing can harm you, and we will constantly be praying for you, and your fellow brothers as you try to rebuild the "A". Take care my friend, and may you stay as warm as possible and may those who pass by your quarters feel the genuine warmth you exude, and are willing to share with anyone who passes through. You, my friend, are a class act, and I want to thank you for allowing us to be part of changing the world for the better. My wife, Susan, has just arrived home and informed me that she was in contact with the kind folks at Colgate who informed her that if you can provide them with an address where the donation will be going, your address in "A", they will be more than happy to consider a possibly quite large donation of toothpaste and brushes. Regardless, just give us the address where you want the stuff sent, and Susan and myself, with the help of God, will send you a gross of brushes and a carton of toothpaste 30-50 tubes, which will be on its way possibly in time for Christmas! Merry Christmas and Happy Holidays and we love you Diggs. Thanks for being YOU!

In Christian love,
David and Susan

10 DEC 2002

Dear Friends and Family,

I just want to reiterate something before we get into this letter. There is a lot going on over here that I cannot write home about. The things I do write about that concern operations are already public news by the time you get this. I am not giving away any classified information. Along those lines, I continue to be amazed by the news stories put out by Pravda (Russian), Al Jazeera (very pro al Qaeda), and...can't remember the name of the Iranian newspaper. All three of these newspapers print fictional stories presented as legitimate news. The latest have been about 16 Special Forces soldiers killed in an ambush (didn't happen) and a mortar accident we had here where they claim U.S. forces were at fault. To my utter amazement, the *Denver Post* actually carried one of these absurd stories without any investigation! Well, thanks for supporting the troops! The *Boston Globe* has also been critical, but that is to be expected.

The holidays are upon us. You can definitely see a change in the morale. The guys are a bit more on edge than usual. Tempers are flaring just a bit quicker, but the good thing is that everyone is aware of the situation and takes it in stride. When the heaters come in, I think a lot of the anxiety will be relieved.

The family support group in Denver sent in a video of the families saying hello to their loved ones. It was a pleasant surprise, and we showed it using a VCR and a video projector. (Very few dry eyes in the room, not to mention on the screen.) It was touching to see how the guys reacted and to see the sincerity of their families.

It appears from what we are seeing here on the TV that the Iraq campaign will be kicking off any day now. I doubt if it will happen before Christmas, but one can never be sure with these things. I am wondering if we will get pulled over there for the follow-up mission when we are finished here.

When I return, I am looking forward to taking my new Harley out for a couple of weeks or so to see Bernie in L.A. and then maybe a ride up Highway One. I really feel the need for a bit of solitude. I'm getting pretty excited about the whole idea, even though it is still more than five months away. Sometimes I catch myself daydreaming about being home; I can already feel the sunshine and the wind in my hair on the bike ride.

One of the other things on my agenda is to visit the schools from where children have been sending correspondence. I am getting some great mail from the kids and have been saving the vast majority of it. I hope to show them photos of the kids here receiving the donations and also to carry a "Thank you" home. I have made it a point to send these school children the typical hat that Afghan boys wear and the scarves the girls wear.

You all have been generous with the cigars, and I, in turn, have been generous with the troops, placing my humidor (yes, I brought it) on my desk for all to partake. It is a big hit. Some of us have started our own cigar club and swap stogies sent from home.

Remember when I asked for toothbrushes and paste? Well, I have been receiving a ton of these to give out to the civilians. The handouts are warmly received by the Afghanis. Man, I'm continually amazed with Americans. God bless you all.

13 DEC 2002

I've had the representative from Brown and Root, the company that is to install our heaters, staying in my room the past two nights. I'm glad he got to feel firsthand what the situation is. We are still two weeks out from having heat.

This morning I was able to put together a few Ziplock® bags of candy (along with toothpaste and toothbrushes) to give out to the children who accompany their merchant parents to the weekly bazaar at our main gate every Friday. The packets were well received. Even the adults asked for a few. The regular kids at the bazaar know me and always want to know if I brought them something. I luckily made 20 packs of toothpaste and candy, and that was the exact amount needed today.

I spent a couple of hours at the bazaar and purchased a second rug from a merchant by the name of Qandi. He invited me to sit with him in his "shop," which is nothing more than an open area with rugs stacked. I felt like a sheik, reclining on a pile of rugs and watching the world go by. The big joke was me calling out to my friends and inviting them into "my shop." The ploy worked, I guess, because Qandi sold three rugs to my buddies. Then I shared tea with the neighboring merchant and gave bags of candy to his sons. Qandi and I ate the local bread and meat dish out of a rolled-up newspaper. I had a big fear of contracting the local version of Montezuma's Revenge, but I didn't want to refuse the hospitality of the locals. When they offer you tea, typically they just take the glass they were drinking from and rinse it out. Filling it once again with tea, it is handed to you with a big smile. Then, with a bit of apprehension, you sip the tea.

By the way, we are expecting our monthly rocket attack any day now. Seems they come around the full moon—the moon providing enough illumination for the bad guys to go about their business. It is no longer perceived as a major threat, but more as a nuisance because we have to get out of bed and man the perimeter. Every once in awhile they get close with the impacts, which tends to keep things interesting.

14 DEC 2002

Mortars are considered guns. The most common we use is 60mm or 81mm; they fire a large round. Hollywood has done a disservice to the mortar. They show mortars firing with a muffled thump, when in reality, they have a large bang after the round slides down the tube and the firing pin strikes the explosive charge. The round travels on a very high trajectory and takes anywhere from a very few seconds to a minute or so to hit the target, depending on the distance of travel. The people on the receiving end of the business will hear the gun being fired; however, while the round is in flight, it doesn't make any noise until it impacts the target. The impact is a surprise, and a good gunner can place rounds in rapid succession on a target. All of our gunners are excellent, and the soldiers we are training are catching on quickly.

I do not recommend the following being distributed to children for reading, as they might find it disturbing.

Today's steady, cold rain mellowed all of our spirits. I'll bet the chaps from England were feeling right at home, and it reminded me of Colorado in the late fall. I was proud to see the Afghanis ready to train this morning, none complaining about the wet or the cold. They are good soldiers.

We had a tragedy today on one of the firing ranges. For weeks since school has been out, the children have been coming out to the ranges to collect brass. They get 10 cents from the local businesses for every pound they gather, which is quite an incentive for them. As boys tend to do, they often defy death while doing stupid stunts. We have had the civil affairs officers out to the local villages to warn the children and their parents about the danger of getting close to the ranges, but to no avail; they still come out to watch and to gather brass. We have resorted to asking the local police to come out and shoo the kids away. Our MPs drive the perimeter and warn anyone they come across. The barbed wire and warning signs that we set out disappear overnight. In short, we have done everything humanly possible to avoid a disaster.

This morning there was a group of eight boys out on our mortar range playing and looking for brass. The boys were escorted off the range and told to go home because we were about to commence firing. The children, ranging in age from 8 to 15, left in the direction of their village but tried once again to enter the range. Again they were ordered to leave the area and were watched until they reached their village.

Unbeknownst to us, they circled around to the backside of the mountain that is our range's backstop. Just before we began firing, they climbed over the top and crept down to a lower elevation, each wanting to be the first one to get brass. Due to the distance involved with firing mortars, they were not spotted by anyone on the range. We fired one red illumination round that hangs from a parachute and acts as a warning to all in the area that the range was "going hot." A few minutes later the crews commenced firing.

The first round apparently landed right in the middle of the kids who were hunkered down behind a large boulder. Of course, no one on the firing line could see any of the action. Of the children, two were able to run to their village, which is over a mile away, and alert the families that there was trouble. The firing continued for several minutes until a car from the village ran a roadblock and drove out to the middle of the range. At that point, all firing ceased. The occupants of the car ran to the spot where the children lay, followed by our men and medical teams.

The first report back to our headquarters was one KIA (killed in action) and three wounded. Minutes later, two KIA, three wounded. Later, three KIA, three wounded. The children were loaded into an ambulance (something we have on every range when in use) and then driven to our compound. The civil affairs officer went to the town to find the parents and escort them to our medical section.

It was such a horrific sight; now four, not three, crumpled little bodies on stretchers—blood everywhere. One survivor had a slight wound to his leg and another needed to be med-evacuated to Bagram for emergency surgery to his face. There was a stunned silence at our camp.

The parents were led in to identify and claim the bodies. It is the custom here to bury the dead before nightfall. Some of the family members were distraught. One man lost his only son, which did not sit well with him. Other family members were stoic. I think the ones who showed little emotion are used to war and death.

The brother of one of the children told us through our interpreter that he had told the kids not to go back to the range. The parents didn't blame us, and that is helping the guys who were in charge of the range handle the situation. I may come across as a bit melodramatic, but I think one of the deceased was one of our English students; it was really hard to tell without the animation associated with a child.

Of course, there will be a big investigation going on with the military, but I don't see any way that the blame can be laid on our men. Everything that might have prevented this tragedy was done.

There is a silence here tonight—no joking, no one outside talking, nothing.

15 DEC 2002

Three of the four dead children were our students.

16 DEC 2002

I don't feel much like writing at the moment, but will do so to get my mind on other things.

Today was pretty much the same as any other, as it seems they all are. I'm now coordinating and planning operations against the bad guys, so my days are pretty much behind a desk.

About 4:00 this afternoon we got a radio call to our headquarters. Two of our soldiers and their interpreter were returning to our base from the palace when someone on the crowded street threw a grenade into their vehicle. The grenade must have rolled in between the two front seats before it detonated. The driver was wounded in his right leg and right side of his head. The passenger had wounds to his left leg and left shoulder. Thank God they had their body armor on; their vests were in tatters. The interpreter, who was in the back seat, suffered an ocular injury but will not lose his eyes. His feet are also full of broken bones, and this will put him in casts and on crutches for months.

Both of our soldiers were taken to the ISAF hospital and went into surgery immediately. One had almost bled out and got to the hospital just in time. The armor saved their lives. They will be going to Germany for more surgery and then home for recovery. Are their military careers over? What awaits them stateside?

As for the bad guys, all three were caught and taken into custody by the Afghanis. The police here have their own way of getting information out of prisoners, and we did not interfere with them. Tomorrow our people will take the prisoners for interrogation. The great thing about this whole situation is that as they tried to escape, they were tackled by the crowd and held until the police came. I've mentioned it before, the people here love Americans, and there are only a few bad apples.

17 DEC 2002

I finally got a good look at the enemy up close. They have such a strong dislike for America and all it stands for, until they are captured; then you are their best friend, and their story usually is that they have been drugged by the Taliban to murder Americans. Our grenade thrower was supposed to commit suicide, but lost his nerve. You can tell when these guys are ready to become martyrs: they shave their entire bodies except their heads, and then they take a bath in preparation for going to meet Allah and the 74 virgins. What a bunch of losers. I'd like to give them all the opportunity to meet Allah, on my own terms. It is amazing to me that the vast majority of the populace support us and our ideals, and still the Taliban and HIG think that with their fundamentalist views they will be the salvation of Afghanistan.

Great news! Sixteen heaters came in today! The bad news is that the installation crew did not come with the heaters. They won't be here for at least a week. We should be having snow in a day or two.

18 DEC 2002

Only seven more shopping days until Christmas. We woke up this morning to a light dusting of snow. We probably got an inch, but it didn't last long, and by about noon everything had melted off. It's okay, though, because we are used to the mud now. But of course, my roof didn't take it well, and once again I'm in a wet bed—not of my own doing, I might add.

Just a few hours ago a suicide bomber blew up across the street. He killed two Afghanis, a French journalist, and himself, of course. (Again, the shaved body.) You just look at what is left of this guy and wonder what on earth was going on in his mind. It is very fortunate that he was kept outside the gate before he detonated himself. What kind of people integrate into their religion the killing of innocent people?

It is beginning to look pretty much like we expected; there is an increase in enemy activity before winter sets in. We will be on our toes for the next few weeks.

19 DEC 2002

This has been a slow day except for an ISAF helicopter crash close by. It was a German aircraft with seven on board, no survivors. The crash was due to mechanical failure. You cannot imagine the magnitude of this crash and the devastation to the personnel on board. The crash site is horrific, with such devastation that the Germans searched a two-mile area thinking one of the crew had fallen out before the impact. Later they discovered the remains of the crew member inside the shattered aircraft.

In the Christmas spirit, I showed the movie "It's a Wonderful Life" tonight. I am surprised by the small turnout with all the events of the past few days. We have had so much trauma around here of late that I would expect to see more people looking for an escape. It will be interesting to see how many people come to the Christmas service.

I'm wondering what sort of Christmas it is going to be in a country where there are some people who want to murder Christians. It clearly will be much different from anything I have experienced in the past, and maybe a bit more significant.

Big on Sunday's agenda is taking several boxes of clothing and toys to an orphanage in downtown Kabul. I, along with several other guys, have volunteered to assist the chaplain in this effort. It will probably take most of the day, starting around 10:00 a.m. We are going to call this "Operation Christmas Blessing."

Must get an early start.

Sincerely,
Diggs

CHAPTER 12
MERRY CHRISTMAS WITH THE USO

Dear Diggs,

I vividly remember Christmas overseas. The advantage of having many men (and women) all in the same situation, along with the fun and food, made it more than bearable. You, my much admired friend, will probably be the catalyst to others' fond Christmas memories!

When you were a puppy, the TV news stations would "report" on the KIAs on each side. If memory serves me, the Vietnamese lost almost 30 million people! In other words, a whole new generation of folks need to learn what to listen to and whom to trust. Wasn't it said "only believe half of what you see and none of what you read"? Lt. Cali (American Division, Mai Li location) would not have been fed to the wolves had it not been for the forward thinking, Fonda inspired U.S. press!

I'm thinking of you every day, my friend. Jesse is on the list, by his request, to receive your e-mails. I read them to my girls here... but frankly have a problem finishing. I get locked up trying to convey what is being said. I am very proud of your service, our flag and country, and the (untapped and fading) American spirit. If you expect anyone else but a Vet to really understand what and why, you're wasting time in the most frustrating manner.

Thank you for your sacrifices and for those of the men and women who stand near you. Christmas will be quickly over... but the VC used to really enjoy this period to hammer the poop outta us! New Year's too...

Watch the concertina wire and keep your head on and in the game.

Love youse,
Paul (ie)

Hey,

Wow. I sat here, just staring at my screen after reading your last e-mail. I wish I could put into words how I feel about what you are going through. I just sit and think, and try to truly appreciate all that you guys are going through. Shame on any of us here for complaining about anything this Christmas season. We are all so lucky. My heater just came on. I am so lucky. I can go shopping today and not worry about being blown up. I am so lucky. Thanks to you guys, that is. It is truly difficult to process and imagine your conditions and your mission. What a tremendous gift you are giving America.

That is awesome what you are doing with the orphanages. I had a lady contact me wanting to get involved with her mission to send toiletries to the orphanages there. She saw the news bit, and wants me to contact Watkins for her. Since Monreal shipped out to hang with you guys, I just gave her the main number and told her to see how they can help, as far as shipping the stuff goes.

Tomorrow is Christmas. Diggs, I wish you could wake up in a nice warm house, drink a nice hot cup of coffee, and enjoy the day. You will always remember Christmas 2002, which is for sure. And, I hope you remember the millions and millions of people you gave a gift to that Christmas. How many people can say that? You are making a difference. A really big and everlasting difference. I hope you realize that, as you are in horrid conditions, freezing your butt off. I feel so inadequate. Please, please tell me if there is ANYTHING I can do, send, or whatever. Please!

I love the pictures you send. Please keep them coming. That one of you in front of the pseudo blackboard that was in the newspaper article was also shown on 9News when they came in. I didn't know you had a VCR, I can send you a copy of the tape if you'd like. You could see all the kids in action, packing up the boxes. Do you want any movies sent???

I know you have limited time to read all your fan mail, so I'll get. I am sending a huge hug to you right now. Have a very merry Christmas tomorrow. I hope all your guys feel the warmth of the

meaning of Christmas tomorrow. I also hope they know we all
think they are Rock Stars back here.
  Be safe Diggs. Merry, Merry Christmas to you!
                            OOXX
                            Michelle

22 DEC 2002

I've mentioned before that the USO has never sent anyone
down to our location. It is almost like we are the "Lost Battalion."
Today we got a last-minute notice via radio that the USO decided
(actually it was Sergeant Major of the Army Jack L. Tilley who
decided) that they were going to send a few entertainers to our
location from Bagram Air Force Base for a two-hour visit. Tonight
there is a big USO show at Bagram, but apparently there was
time to get these folks down to see us. This unexpected visit
threw a monkey wrench into my plans to go to the orphanage to
hand out goodies, but there were enough guys who volunteered
to help that I could stay behind and fulfill my position as Protocol
Officer. Our guests were: Karri Turner from the TV show "JAG,"
Kathy Griffin from "Suddenly Susan," John Layfield "Bradshaw"
who is a WWF wrestler, Darryl Worley who is a rising star on
the country singing circuit, along with their managers and two
cheerleaders from the football team Jacksonville Jaguars. I only
had three hours to put together an agenda for them before they
arrived.

Our guests flew in on a Blackhawk helicopter and landed on
the landing zone (LZ) in our compound. I met them at the pad
and escorted them a few feet away to brief them on their tour
agenda. There eyes were as big as saucers and they were clearly
taken aback because they had just flown over a vastly devastated
portion of this country. I think the condition of our compound
and the squalor we have been living in was totally unexpected.
It was much different from the Air Force bases they had visited
previously. To make matters worse, they had to fly in over the

site where the German helicopter crashed a few days ago. Now there is an eye opener!

I gave them a quick briefing of our missions (both combat and training the Afghan army), and then I answered their questions. The majority of the questions dealt with the local populace, the poverty level, and the devastation that surrounded us. I told them about the English classes that Chaplain Andy and I teach, the fundraising, school supply donations coming in, and the food and clothing donations we were going to be making to the orphanage later in the day. They were clearly impressed, and one of the managers asked for my e-mail so he could talk to the "Hollywood types" who are always looking for a charity. I hope he comes through.

After the quick briefing and chat with our MP security element, I escorted our guests through the concertina gate that separates the helipad and the Afghan army barracks. (Concertina is the coiled barbed wire that is placed on top of walls and fences for security.) I should note that when helicopters come in, the Afghan soldiers gather on the hilltop and at the gate to see who arrives. Some of the celebrities were anxious to talk to the Afghan soldiers, and there were plenty on hand to meet them. I think I've mentioned before that the Afghanis love to have their picture taken. Today was no exception, especially with the cheerleaders who were dressed modestly. Keep in mind that the Afghanis don't own cameras, but they wanted our guests to take pictures with them using our guests' cameras—to create photos the Afghanis would never see. Does that make sense?

Once we made our way through the surging Afghanis, we reached the interior gate to our compound where the orphanage convoy was gearing up to go. The timing was perfect because the guys and gals who volunteered to be on the convoy had a chance to meet our guests. It was amazing to see who each of them was interested in meeting. Everyone had their favorites, and the cameras were just clicking away. The celebrities were surrounded by soldiers who were starved for attention and anything to break up the monotony. You could see everyone's spirits rising. I think it was an extremely emotional experience for our guests because they had never been in this situation.

After about 30 minutes it was time for the convoy to depart for the orphanage, and I escorted our guests to the medical facility (what we call the Med Shed) where our docs were giving some of the men rabies shots. I made sure they met Doc Enzenhauer who does all the eye surgeries on the children. Kind of funny, the guys who were getting the shots volunteered to get them so they could meet the celebrities. It worked; they did get to spend time with our guests.

After the Med Shed, we did a quick tour of the mess hall (oops, dining facility), and then we went to a weapons display to give them a chance to put their hands on all sorts of captured weapons. Of course, there was a quick stop at the Bombay Lounge for photos in front of our Christmas bush and lighted tank. We finished the tour with a stop at three blown-up Taliban tanks that are on the far side of our compound. Our guests climbed aboard a tank and had their photos made, and then it was time to go.

I think the things that made the greatest impact on our guests are the Spartan living conditions, the fact that we are all citizen soldiers, the length of the deployment away from families, our professional attitude, and the fact that we are compassionate and are doing the "hearts and minds" types of missions. I am positive that it is a trip they will long remember. I am also positive that their visit gave us a tremendous morale boost.

Before they boarded the aircraft, I told our guests what a profound impact they had on our soldiers, and some of the guests mentioned that they would rather stay at our compound than go to the "luxurious" Bagram Air Force Base for the show that evening. A couple of them got misty-eyed when they told me they are grateful for what we are doing for them and the country. I think it was a good experience for all involved. We said our goodbyes and they boarded the helicopter. As it lifted into the sky, I could see them waving goodbye. Then, in a cloud of dust, they were gone.

As for "Operation Christmas Blessing," we gave the orphanage over two tons of food, 900 backpacks, and boxes upon boxes of clothing. Some of the kids had no shoes, some had the wrong size, and some had mismatched pairs. The warm clothes will go a long way. We also gave them candy and wished them a Merry Christmas. The Afghanis know about Christmas, although they do not celebrate it. They believe that Jesus was a prophet, but not the Son of God. There were over 1,000 children at this orphanage and there are an estimated 1 million orphans in Afghanistan. The kids at these orphanages will never be adopted; no one can afford to do so. They stay until they are 18 and then are out on their own. At least at the orphanage they get a roof over their heads, an education, and warm meals.

Tonight some children of expatriates came and sang carols to us at our compound. I have never heard such a sweet sound. It is going to be a wonderful Christmas.

To all my family and friends, I am wishing you a very Merry Christmas and the best for the New Year! See you in a few months.

Love and peace,
Diggs

CHAPTER 13
MOVING TO BAGRAM

Diggs,

So I take it you're not getting any skiing in this year?

But on a serious note, I was so touched by your letters. I am proud of what you are doing in Afghanistan and what you represent over there. I remember a phrase that says "Because I have been given much, I too must give." That is why America is over there. And you represent the best of what we stand for. (Not sure about the Republicans controlling both the House and the Senate). If there is anything I can do to help, please let me know.

Your insight into their world helps put meaningless, petty problems into perspective. I appreciate your thoughts. Take care of yourself and your men. Write when you can.

Pat

26 DEC 2003

Dear Family and Friends,

We all realize that the old adage, "All work and no play makes Jack a dull boy," is true. It is really remarkable to see the variety of things people have done to raise their spirits. The constant threat of death tends to keep people on the edge, which needs to be dulled in some way. One company built a huge fire pit, and in the evenings they sit around the roaring fire and chat. Another team has built a mini-theatre in their hooch and are currently into the 20th episode of the "Sopranos." A lot of the guys have established friendships with the soldiers from different countries, and they have dinner together at the different compounds on a semi-monthly basis. The MPs (I admire them for their esprit de corps) had a Christmas celebration in their area, complete with fire pit roasted turkey and eggnog. And, of course, we have the

Fabulous Bombay Lounge with the weekly movies. I was going to have a New Year's soirée in my room for a select few; however, I am being sent to Bagram Air Force Base to work in the operations area. My plans will have to be put off for another time; hopefully, not until next New Year!

I have given much thought to the soldiers I work with who have families and have missed the holidays with them. I cannot imagine what is going through their minds. Although some come and talk to me about their concerns, it is still not within my scope to understand, even though I also felt a bit of depression over Christmas. Just one minute with my parents, sisters, nieces, nephew, and brothers-in-law at our annual Christmas gathering would have been a splendid moment. I shared Christmas with my family through the Internet, which made things easier.

I have noticed a drop in my weight. I'm down about 15 pounds to somewhere around 174. It is hard to get an accurate measurement, so this is a guess. Believe me, while I feel good at this weight, I don't recommend the diet. My hair has turned almost entirely gray during this trip, but I guess I'm lucky it hasn't all fallen out.

I forgot to mention that during the Christmas holidays we received many letters from different elementary schools, as well as bushel baskets of cards. There are cards written by people of all ages and addressed to "To any U.S. Soldier." It's great to know that the people at home are thinking of us. Some of the cards are obviously written by individuals who are senior citizens. I wonder if they fought in the previous wars or lost loved ones in those wars. Maybe this is just their way of contributing to the effort. We see a number of cards that were written by the same individual. To think that someone spent the enormous amount of time and effort to write multiple cards is amazing. No matter what the circumstance, all are appreciated.

Some of the letters from kids are a hoot! "Kill anyone named Azhir or Osama," and "Thanks a lot for being there for me. If I was there I would have peed my pants and went running. But you are brave and you will step in front of me and protect me."

Their letters are compelling. They are full of innocence and a lack of understanding as to what is going on here. Of course, there are a lot of individuals who have never experienced all the emotions involved with being on this side of a weapon. Have I mentioned lately that there are people here who want to kill us?

I've been given less than 12 hours notice that I will be going up to Bagram Air Force Base to work in the operations center. This has kind of upset me, not so much for the mission, but because of the short notice. I'm going to have to spend a lot of time packing my gear and preparing for the move when I should be sleeping.

Bagram is the hub of the war. All the decisions are made there, so I am honored that I'm being sent to work in the main operations center. I know I've mentioned before what a good life they have there, and compared to Kabul, it is true. I guess it is more of a trade-off; you give some, you gain some. I will now have hot water and heat in my tent, but the trade-off will be the quality of the food.

It is said by the guys here who have spent time in Bagram that it is hell—purgatory being where I am currently located. Bagram has over 5,000 soldiers on a small compound. I've made several trips there on business and have noticed that it is extremely dusty due to the amount of traffic on the few roads, extremely noisy due to the flight line, and extremely crowded. As I've mentioned before about the PX, it takes over an hour just to get in, and another 20 minutes to check out. The bright side is: THERE IS A PX. The soldiers live in large tents, but I hear that the tents have wooden floors and HEATERS! The down side is the food. Whereas at Kabul our mess soldiers had pride in their work and went out of their way to make things bearable, the cooks at Bagram could care less. The food at Bagram is pitiful.

27 DEC 2002

We left KMTC this morning in a convoy of several trucks. I rode with three other soldiers in the back of a cargo HMVEE that had a canvas shell. Our breath was forming condensation on the canvas and, due to the cold, ice fell like snowflakes every time we hit a bump. The convoys are a bit risky at the moment because of the threat of attack. I did not like riding in the canvas-covered compartment, as it would make the opportunity to return fire, if fired upon, very difficult. Needless to say, we all wore armor and helmets.

Bagram is quite small, surrounded with Hesco walls and concertina wire. In case I haven't mentioned Hesco walls before, they are canvas and wire collapsible boxes that are filled with sand and dirt, and they create quite an impregnable obstacle. A wall can be thrown up in a matter of minutes and filled rapidly if you have a front-end loader. They vary in height from three feet to ten feet. I would like to be heir to the Hesco fortune, as I am sure this guy has made billions. Hesco walls are everywhere; they have replaced sandbags for the most part. What a great idea!

Bagram is regulation military. The 82nd Airborne is running the operations in Afghanistan. They are the quintessential strack (strictly by the rules and regulations) military unit. Haircuts, uniform, and regulations are enforced to the maximum. This is not a bad thing, unless you are an unconventional warrior as we are in Special Forces. On Bagram you can get a ticket for jaywalking, not using a seatbelt, not having the proper uniform...and the list goes on and on. Now, let me tell you about military tickets. I've never had one, but I hear all that happens is your superiors are informed that you are breaking regulations and they deal with you.

One of the real beefs between Special Forces and the 82nd is the fact that we have the black fleece jackets that were issued to SF units. It is really a great piece of equipment and keeps us warm. However, the majority of the 82nd don't have the fleece, so we can't wear ours outside of our small compound unless we wear them under our uniforms, and of course, they don't fit under the uniform.

Another sticking point here is saluting. As SF, we do not salute because it identifies the officers as the targets. The 82nd wants enlisted men to salute officers, so it is obvious that the second man returning the salute is the officer. When they salute an officer, they sound off with "Airborne!" In the typical military fashion, officers should respond "All the way!" Way too many soldiers have saluted me today, and when they sound off with "Airborne, sir," I return their salute and respond with a hushed "Sniper Check!" This really throws them and is kind of fun. Of course, they don't say anything back to me and wander off on their merry way.

Upon arrival I was dropped off at the tent I am going to occupy. Within the tent the guys have done a bunch of work and have actually built plywood rooms within—and there is heat! I now have a room that is about a quarter of the size of my room at KMTC (actually just enough room to turn around in), but there is heat and no rocket hole in the ceiling over my bed. The guys here are a good crew, and I haven't seen them in a month or two. They were thrilled to see me, and I find that quite flattering. I should mention that many of the enlisted guys, as well as the officers, address me as Diggs or Captain Diggs. It is very rare that someone uses the term "sir," and that is how I like it because I call them all by their first names.

28 DEC 2002

I had my first real day of work. I was introduced at the day's morning update briefing as Captain Brown, founder of the Bombay Lounge. What a hoot. The atmosphere here is so relaxed even though momentous decisions are made on a regular basis. I settled into work and got a lot accomplished in my eight-hour shift. Yes, you heard correctly, eight hours! Holy cow! I forgot to mention that I had a hot shower this morning! My first truly hot shower in three months! Where previously I'd been limited to one shower every four days, I had a long (five minute) shower today. Not only that, I had one this evening after I ran four miles and worked out at the semi-gym. Two showers in one day! I think I washed most of three months of dirt out of my pores today, although I am sure there is more where that came from. Okay, it is not heaven, but it is a nice change. When running, we stay on base and carry our pistols while we run on the outer perimeter. There is always the chance that someone will take a pot-shot at us.

There was a box waiting in the post office here from a friend in Ohio with a few exquisite cigars and about a dozen pairs of fleece sleeping socks (Toasty Toes) his wife made. I made it a point to hand these out to the guys immediately. The men really appreciated the socks. Each of them made it a point to tell me how toasty their feet were, mine included! I also handed out a box of cigars that my father sent. Everyone is a happy camper. Another thing of interest, all the good things happen at the headquarters, or as we say, around the "flagpole." Well, they have tons of boxes of goodies here that have never made it down to our location. I've never seen so much snack food, personal hygiene items, etc., in one location.

I imagine the journal from Bagram will be a bit boring as compared to Kabul. I also want to mention that the e-mail here is extremely slow due to the amount of bandwidth used on this base. It typically takes 10 minutes just to log on and retrieve a single letter, so if my e-mails diminish during my stay here, that is the reason.

One of the first things I did this evening was to install red chili pepper Christmas lights around the door to our tent. Bagram is pitch black in the night and you literally cannot see your hand in front of your face. The red lights on our tent can be spotted among the rows of tents and help us find our way much easier. The lights do not give off enough light to pose any enemy targeting opportunities.

Time for shut-eye. Wow, a warm bunk!

Cheers!
Diggs

CHAPTER 14
VERY BAD PEOPLE OUT THERE

Covenant, O Sister...

to make their women widows and their children orphans.

Covenant, O Sister...

to make them desire death and hate appointments and prestige.

Covenant, O Sister...

to slaughter them like lambs and let the Nile and Euphrates rivers flow with their blood.

Covenant, O Sister...

to be a pick of destruction for every godless and apostate regime."

(from al Qaeda training literature)

29 DEC 2002

During my stay in Afghanistan I have had the opportunity to read translated documents published by Osama bin Laden and the Taliban. Part of the documents state that their goal is to slaughter the infidels; that is you and me and our families. These people are truly barbaric. There will be no negotiated peace with them. There will be no appeasing them.

Here are excerpts from some of the documents, along with my thoughts:

The confrontation that we are calling for (Jihad) with the apostate regimes does not know Socratic debates...Platonic ideals...nor Aristotelian diplomacy. But it knows the dialogue of bullets, the ideals of assassination, bombing, and destruction, and the diplomacy of the cannon and machine-gun.

It is not just America they target, but all Christians, no matter where they live. This is evident on a daily basis with the

Christians being killed regularly in Kashmir, India, Indonesia, the Philippines, and elsewhere. Beware, they will show no mercy. This goes for the Iraqis, also. I'm sick to my stomach that people like the actor Sean Penn would even consider going to Iraq and then lecture us that the Iraqi government is a peace-loving government. Of course, you will have the Ed Asners, and what's his name (the guy from the TV show M*A*S*H) who are talking trash about our country and the thought that we are warmongers. These guys don't have a clue. I wonder just where they get their ideas. Have them spend a week here and maybe, just maybe, they will have their eyes opened. Let them spend a week here witnessing the suffering that the Taliban and al Qaeda have brought upon this part of the world. Of course, they will never come here to see the truth; why leave the comfort of their mansions when they can spew deceit from a secure television studio? They are just actors who live in fantasy worlds and make an income from it—always keep that in mind.

> Islamic governments have never and will never be established through peaceful solutions and cooperative councils. They are established as they (always) have been: by pen and gun, by word and bullet, by tongue and teeth.

The bad guys have no qualms about suicide attacks. It is whatever it takes to kill the infidel. In fact, they believe that if they die killing you and your family, they will be granted heaven. They bribe the poor, the lame, and the mentally deranged with money. If they kill an American, they will receive $10,000; if they die in the process, it will be $20,000. Imagine this in a world where the average annual income is less than $500. The planners prefer suicide bombings so that no information can be gotten out of a captured prisoner. Those who are not willing to die for Allah use money to buy martyrs. The true Muslims will tell you that killing like this is sacrilege, but still there are those who are willing to die for whatever deranged reason.

These young men realized that an Islamic government would never be established except by the bomb and rifle. Islam does not coincide or make a truce with unbelief, but rather confronts it.

Pay attention people; it's coming, if not already here. We are in the beginning of a war that is going to change the face of the world.

The young men came to prepare themselves for Jihad commanded by the majestic Allah's order in the holy Koran. Against them make ready your strength to the utmost of your power, including steeds of war, to strike terror into the hearts of the enemies of Allah and your enemies, and others besides whom ye may not know, but whom Allah doeth know.

CHAPTER 15
NEW YEAR'S IN THE "BIG A"

Dear Captain Diggs, or do I call you Captain Brown?

You don't know me. My name is Sharon Rheinhart. A friend of mine passed your e-mails on to me. She has received them from someone else who forwarded them on to her.

I am so happy to hear that things are not as bad as the press would lead us to believe. My husband has been activated to go to war. Our family has been very concerned about the situation, but after reading your e-mails we can sleep easier at night. Our children think you are a hero, as they do their father.

Thank you for sharing your thoughts with us back home and explaining the reality of what is happening.

Sincerely,
Sharon

30 DEC 2002

The Kabul team has just recovered another MEDCAP mission. This mission sent two doctors, a dentist, and two veterinarians to a tiny village on the Pakistani border. They saw over 300 patients in one day! The highlights of the trip were delivering a baby boy and saving the life of a severely malnourished six-month-old girl. It is really amazing to think just how a little help can go a long way.

Where I am working, I hear all the radio traffic and see the goings on. Every day it seems that there is some kid somewhere who has had an eye or limb destroyed playing with an unexploded ordinance (UXO). The UXOs are left over from years of fighting in Afghanistan. The U.S. Army is flying these kids in for emergency surgery on a regular basis. If this isn't "winning the hearts and minds" of the locals, nothing is. Actually, the attacks on American soldiers drop off dramatically in regions where this effort has been made. I can't recall the Taliban ever taking care of someone's children.

The eye doctor has had his hands full with surgeries. One little girl had her eye blown out after playing with a UXO. There was really nothing Doc could do for her because it took over three days to find her and get her to our hospital. Since in this country you can't find glass eyes, we went to town and bought an assortment of marbles to find the right size to fill the socket, and then he sewed skin over it. Without the marble, she would be left with a sunken eye socket. It is sad. Doc says there are a lot of eyes he could save, but the equipment he needs just doesn't exist here.

The poor children in this country; every day is a struggle. For the most part they play until they are four years old, then they must start to contribute to the household chores. I've seen kids carrying buckets of water and stacks of twigs as big as they are. The lucky ones go to school. The real lucky ones get to stay in school past the age of 13. There are so many kids playing and begging in the street. Their toys consist of kites, bricks on a string, and cans. On occasion you will see a doll, but that is rare. You do see many toy guns. Many of the children help their parents in the market, and many more work in the field. I wonder what the future holds for them.

Another interesting thing about the families here is that when a daughter marries, she moves in with her husband and his family. The son brings the bride home to help support the family. The eldest son helps his father support the family and becomes the leader of the family when the father dies. Many marriages are prearranged. A man may take up to four wives. He must pay a dowry to the bride's family, and according to my interpreter the dowry can range in price from a few livestock up to $10,000. The women are truly oppressed here, but for some it is a way of life they have always endured, and they see no subjugation. Many still wear the burka even though it is not enforced with beatings as it was with the Taliban in power.

There is a lot of fighting going on that you aren't hearing about at home. If the Iraq war kicks off, I wonder if you will hear anything at all about Afghanistan. I just finished reading three different newspaper articles via the Internet about a skirmish that occurred yesterday. Each article had a different perspective on the incident. Only one (American) was close to the truth. The Islamic newspaper was totally distorted, of course.

Sometimes I feel overwhelmed with all of the events that are happening. It seems that there is something dramatic going on all the time. I am writing this letter at midnight, and there has been a steady stream of jets taking off for some distant location. The intermittent roar of the jet engines has made sleep next to impossible.

31 DEC 2002

Chaplain Andy from Kabul has been brought to the hospital on Bagram AFB suffering from pneumonia. I will try and get by to see him tomorrow. This has been a slow day all around.

01 JAN 2003

I made it over to the German compound last night to ring in the New Year. They had an assortment of traditional German food and, of course, German beer. It was a small gathering and by invitation only. The entertainment was hilarious. They had a group of guys behind a hanging sheet with holes cut in it for their arms. Each arm had a sock puppet on, and these puppets lip-synced (can a sock puppet lip-sync?) some classical songs. Later, a guy dressed in a burka came out and did an exotic dance. At midnight the Germans set off three "flash bang" hand grenades. The flash bang is an extremely loud and bright explosive that is used to disorient the enemy in a non-lethal fashion. Unfortunately, the Germans neglected to tell the post command that they were going to do this and there were guys all over the base rolling out of their tents thinking we were being attacked. The MPs came by and everything was calmed. I didn't stay late because I had the early shift in the morning. I will say that it was a nice break from the doldrums.

Chaplain Andy was released from the hospital today so I missed the opportunity to see him. I hear he is okay and that he actually had carbon monoxide poisoning from a cheap heater he bought in town. Still no heaters at our base in Kabul.

In the late afternoon several guys from KMTC dropped by my hooch to tell me that I am sorely missed. The major who sent me here has also dropped in to tell me that I'll be going back sooner than he had planned. I feel that is a good thing; I wish to fight the war with my brothers. To quote Shakespeare in Henry V, "We few, we happy few, we band of brothers; for he today that sheds his blood with me shall be my brother...."

Happy New Year everyone!

Cheers!

Diggs

CHAPTER 16
AFGHAN OVERFLIGHT

Diggs,

 Carol Williams Bailey brought the hat that you sent me last night and words cannot begin to express the joy and happiness that the hat brought with it. We haven't seen each other in so many years and for you to have thought enough of our friendship thrills me to no end. Your gift will very probably be the gift that brings my old heart the true joy of the season. I cannot imagine any other gift that will come close. My kids think the hat is darn cool too.

 To fill you in: I'm a folliclely challenged person (bald) and frequently wear straw hats in the summer for shade and wool hats for warmth in the winter. Literally, when Carol brought the hat by, I was in the barn with my hat on. So it will get much use, really. I even wore it to work today. (Don't get too confused about my barn. We have a foosball table, ping-pong table, as well as my daughter's new drums. Also, I have an office in the barn. The point being, it is not a barn for horses and cows.)

 Recently I have read much about WWII and have developed a great sense of respect for the military. Your service to our country and the help it renders in me maintaining my cherished freedoms is greatly appreciated. Thank you. Please be safe and lucky. Continue the good work and know that you and your family are in my heart and prayers.

Wishing you the best with
my fondest regards,
Butch

07 JAN 2003

Dear Friends and Family,

 I have just returned from the far southeastern corner of Afghanistan. At the moment this is the hot spot, although my current base was rocketed twice and took sporadic machine gun fire the night before I left. The sieve-like border between Afghanistan and Pakistan allows many of the bad guys to slip through to attack our compounds, then retreat back to sanctuary on the Pakistani side. We will just have to see how much longer this will be tolerated.

Part of my adventure included a lot of air travel, both by the workhorse of the Air Force (the four engine, prop-driven, C-130 Hercules transport plane) and an assortment of helicopters. The helicopters were the big twin rotary C-47 Chinook transport and the UH-60 Blackhawk, mainstay of the Army Air Wing.

When a C-130 comes in for a landing, many times the passengers who will be boarding must do a "hot load." This is where the aircraft continues to run its engines and the tailgate is dropped. They board the plane after fighting their way though the blinding dust and the prop wash, which is like a blast furnace. This is a very common way of boarding a military plane or helicopter. The C-130 has nylon bench seats that fold down from the walls. It is not at all comfortable, but then it isn't made for comfort, it is made for efficiency. The funny thing about flying either in the plane or helicopter is that folks usually fall asleep almost immediately upon being seated. I'm not sure if it is the steady hum (which is quite loud) or anxiety, but it happens.

This mission was the first time I was actually up in the air for a view of the countryside. It is even more desolate than I imagined. In your mind, pick out the most barren part of the U.S. you have seen and then multiply that by 100. I am positive I've seen places that no man has been. I will add, however, that on this trip I did see greenery, and that was totally surprising. Of course, we were farther south and there were streams and rivers, but not many.

Afghanistan from the air and over the mountains brings to mind a sea of snow-covered peaks as far as you can see. The mountains hold very few trees. The few that exist are in the valleys along the now frozen streams. Occasionally there will be a mud house along the tributary, but no road leading to it. I wonder just what the residents do during the winter. They can't get out, and there isn't any agriculture occurring. Do they just "hibernate" in their huts with no TV, no stores anywhere nearby, and no electricity?

Here is what happened on my trip:

On January 3, I was ordered on short notice to depart for a distant location. With what little time I had, I threw my gear together and headed to the airfield. It was 0400 (4:00 a.m.), the air was brisk, to say the least, and I was beginning to wonder if I had on enough layers of clothing. To get on this flight, it was necessary for me to "bump" a guy who was going on leave. I felt a bit of remorse about shorting his leave, but I had priority with my mission. There was another flight for him later that day.

I've mentioned before about the MEDCAP missions we perform. When our docs are out in the remote villages and they find someone in a life threatening condition, we will fly them to our hospitals and hopefully save their life. I was accompanied on this flight by a 12-year-old girl named Razoka. She had died after suffering from a variety of symptoms for weeks before our docs found her. I'm not a medic, so bear with me. According to the medical report that accompanied her, she had a salmonella bacterial infection for 10 weeks, meningitis for eight weeks, and a perforated ileum for four weeks. Razoka rode in a brushed aluminum transport coffin with two carrying handles on each side, pressured sealed—such a big container for such a little girl. I thought to myself, *Someone's baby girl is coming home.* Unfortunately, not everyone who seeks treatment is saved.

The lack of quality medical attention in Afghanistan would blow your mind. Think of any minor ailment you have had (a fever, an infection, appendix, tonsils…you name it) that could have resulted in your death had it not been treated by modern medicine. These people live with the threat of death daily from the most minor incident, not to mention war. It is a very hard life for them, and every day is a struggle. I am growing weary from witnessing so much death.

07 JAN 2003

My return home...gosh, did I call it "home?" I know I've been here too long now. My return to *base* was all rotary wing. I found this very rewarding. Although the flight took four times as long as the C-130, I could actually observe more on the ground.

With the rotary wing aircraft we flew at a much lower altitude due to the elevation of our location. Helicopters must have thick air for lift, and the thin air at the high altitude makes flight difficult. Most of our flight was 200 feet above the ground.

Looking down on the land, there were mud villages scattered randomly and sparsely throughout the land. Some of the villages consist of four or five huts, others as many as twenty. There are all different styles, depending on the wealth of the village. I believe this must be determined by their source of water and the resulting crops they can grow (beyond their meager needs) and then sell. The huts vary from single-room squares with a domed mud ceiling to the more elaborate multi-room houses with mud-wall compound. The mud is either mud brick covered with mud plaster or simply mud. The walls are usually three feet thick, and the composition is mud and straw, unless they have the resources to buy fire-baked bricks. Where I am now, there are no fire-baked bricks. Many of the villages do not have electricity. The huts all face east to catch the morning heat in the winter and block the intense western heat in the summer. The thick walls actually make them heating and cooling efficient. You'd also be amazed to know that it takes a mighty powerful projectile to penetrate these walls.

As we flew above these villages in the early morning light, the inhabitants came out to see our *chalk*. Chalk is aviator talk for the formation. We were in two Blackhawks, one Chinook, and an Apache gunship for escort. The villagers waved and the kids came out and gave the "thumbs up" just as they do when we drive by in Kabul. I wondered what they were thinking down there. ("Another war. Who is it this time? Are these good guys or bad guys?") As far out as we are, you can rest assured that the majority of the people have no idea about 9/11 or the current situation. I wonder if they ever dream about flying and seeing another part of the world. So many of these people will never be more than a few miles from their homes in their entire lives. Many of the villages have only single-track, well-worn paths leading to them or leading away from them. That tells me they do not have modern transportation. The primitive nature of life below is almost biblical in its nature.

The "moonscape" of Afghanistan seems to go on forever.

Flocks of sheep were pinned in their mud circular enclosures for protection during the night. They had just enough room to turn around. Below us a dog chased our helicopter for a few feet and then returned to its master's compound, self-assured that it had scared us off.

We flew over both single-track and double-track paths. Somewhere out there automobiles exist, although we have yet to see any. The roads and trails go on endlessly to the horizon, apparently with no destination.

There were what appeared to be bomb craters making a lazy zigzag for a mile or so. I saw this pattern again and again. I finally realized that these are wells that have been dug to follow the underground aquifer. How long does it take to dig these wells? How long to build a house with a mud wall by hand? I guess these people have nothing but time. They don't have a favorite TV show to watch or a bridge game to go to. Kids aren't going to school. It's highly unlikely that they are going to take a break and run down the corner to Starbucks®.

We flew over what at one time must have been a vast, shallow lake. The sand was almost white, and toward the middle was a bit of water. There were wells dug over a wide range, with single-track trails leading to each. It is obvious that as one well dries up another is dug.

Looking out the windows on the port side (left) was the great nothingness. To the starboard side (right) mountain peaks covered in snow loomed above us and were so close that I thought I could touch them. We made a hard bank to the right and cut through a pass. A few minutes later we passed over the remnants of a fort that must have been built when the British were here over 130 years ago. The six-sided and turreted walls have withstood the wind and erosion of time, and they show little wear. A minute later we passed over one of our firebases. (These are bases of operation in remote locations.) Will our firebase be standing a hundred years from now, and what will the history books say about our foray into Afghanistan?

Four hours later I was back at my base awaiting the next call. I was notified that the commanding general (two-star) has requested that I work for him. His e-mail read, "This man is a genius." I thought it was a joke at first, but as it turns out, the offer is legitimate. I will have to give this some thought. Who knows what the future holds and the influences from the choices we make? I will meet with him in a week or so to discuss the options. I am glad I have choices.

I am going to watch the DVD "Lawrence of Arabia" again tonight. It is my favorite movie and a gift from Jeanie and Jerry Perkins in Duncan, Oklahoma. I can't tell you how many times in my life I've viewed this movie. Lawrence was a brilliant man and tactician. He led the Arabs in the fight against the Turks in World War I. After my father and uncle, T.E. Lawrence is one of my heroes. Giving it some thought, I am almost living Lawrence's life now—in a desolate land, building an army out of multicultural tribes. This movie should be mandatory viewing for anyone in the military, especially the unconventional warrior.

Today we heard a loud and nearby explosion. The engineers destroy a lot of UXO (unexploded ordinance) by detonation, but this explosion was louder than usual and had everyone's attention. It turns out that one of the MPs stepped on a land mine within the base compound! He lost his right leg and hand. Even in "safe areas" there is danger. This is such a large base that I have no idea who the kid is, but it seems most of the MPs who are on guard duty are the kids. What a shame! I pray he recovers quickly and makes the most out of his life.

CHAPTER 17
THE THINGS WE TAKE FOR GRANTED

Hi Diggs,

My name is Ann Iungerich and I am Jeri Custer's sister-in-law. We met at Laurie and Bryan's at Labor Day or was it Memorial Day last year or was it before that? Dave and I have four boys ages 19-6 and several of them were with us that day.

Anyway, Jeri has been forwarding your letters to me. I have enjoyed reading your side of the story. I know that what I hear or read in the media is so biased. Thanks for all you are doing! Please thank all the men around you too. We are so thankful for men like you to help keep the U.S.A. free.

God bless ya!!
Ann

11 JAN 2003

Wow! I can't believe the PX here has the DVD set "Band of Brothers." For those of you who don't know what I'm talking about, it is based on the book by Stephen Ambrose of same the title. Basically, Easy Company, 2nd Battalion, 506th PIR, 101st Airborne Division, invades Europe during World War II. It is a true story, with Tom Hanks and Steven Spielberg collaborating much as they did in "Saving Private Ryan." It is an excellent series that I didn't see when it previewed on HBO. Movies like these really make you appreciate the *Greatest Generation*. They give perspective on just how pale my situation is to theirs, in comparison. Truly, World War II was the last "romantic war" with Glenn Miller, the classic movies and songs, and an entire nation united in a just cause.

The helicopters have been flying all night. As the moon becomes full, the enemy picks up their operational tempo. I hate to say this, but I am beginning to view the enemy much as I do roaches. They come out of their caves at night and attempt to wreak havoc. If you have seen roaches scatter when the light comes on, Taliban and al Qaeda are the same. Sometimes I feel there is just no end in sight. I am truly upset that these guys have interrupted peace on the planet for their sick interpretation of how they think everyone else should live. Just when it appears that humanity is on the verge of a peaceful existence, diseases are eradicated, world hunger is on the verge of being solved, and compassion abounds, something like this has to pop up. My feelings are the same toward the North Koreans and Iraqis. On occasion I will see gun camera footage from our aircraft, and I begin to realize it is just a matter of time before the bad guys lose.

This whole situation reminds me, as it should you, that every generation has its villains that must be dealt with swiftly and without mercy. Hitler, Stalin, Kim Li Jung, Hussein, and Osama bin Laden all should have been eliminated before things got out of control. Unfortunately, the Clinton White House could not and would not handle the bin Laden situation in its infancy, and now we have to deal with this on a grand scale. I am ashamed of how William Jefferson Clinton mismanaged our country's security.

I'm stunned…I just got off the Internet where I received word that my uncle died. Another of the *Greatest Generation* gone. Sad day here. My "brothers" here with me have left their posts to spend time with me and express their condolences. I'm crushed. Otis was a great man who served his country with honor and dignity. I shall miss him.

12 JAN 2003

Today Chaplain Andy and three of my friends came up from Kabul to see me. I'm taking everything in stride. I'm glad to see them; they are long-lost brothers. I decided to work the rest of the day and then spend some time by myself.

Another box of cigars came in today from a friend of a friend. This, on top of the other boxes that have come from stateside recently, has given me an ample supply that I share with the rest of the troops. They are all good, but I am holding the best to take back to Kabul when I see my fellow unit members. While I'm living a much easier life here than I was two weeks ago, I am anxious to get back "home" with my guys.

Thanks to everyone who has been so generous and thoughtful, too many to mention here, but you know who you are. The gifts just keep coming in—a variety of items that put a smile on all faces. War is not won by military strength alone, but by a common effort that includes support from home.

We took up a collection today to help defray the expenses of the wife of one of our guys who was injured in a rocket incident. He is now stateside and will be undergoing multiple facial reconstructions. She has flown to Walter Reed Army Hospital to stay with him. Hopefully, the money we have collected will cover most of her expenses. They are both in our prayers.

13 JAN 2003

A very pleasant surprise tonight: Outback Steakhouse sponsored dinner for the entire garrison. This is the first real steak I have had in over three months. The little girl (little, ha...20-something) who was serving the meal told me that over 4,000 employees volunteered to come here, but they only allowed 16 to make the trip. This has been a real eye-opener for her. My sincere thanks to Outback. If you ever dine at one of these establishments, please pass my thanks along.

Going back to the families of the children who were accidentally killed on our mortar range, a few days ago Chaplain Andy and another representative from the military met with the families of the four children. Andy keeps me up-to-date on all the goings on in Pol-e-charkhi. The meeting went extremely well with no hard feelings.

This is what the village elder had to say (paraphrased):

We have had many children killed over the past 20 years. We have not had any peace until the Americans came. It is so important that you stay and stabilize our country. The children will be missed, but your contribution, the fact that your soldiers are away from their families and friends, is more than enough compensation.

(Wow! And the Taliban think the people want them back here!)

The families will be compensated monetarily for their loss. We are going to place a plaque on the newly refurbished classroom where I taught these kids English, dedicating the remodeling in their honor. I wish I could be there for the ceremony, but alas, it is not meant to be. I can't believe I have such a strong emotional bond with the children of this country, not having kids of my own. I wish I could bring them all to America, if just for a moment. It won't happen; these children are destined to remain here the rest of their lives. A few may venture beyond the borders of this country. Hopefully, they will keep happy memories of the Americans for the remainder of their lives, and they will pass that memory on to their children. I believe this is why all the Europeans I am dealing with love America. After World War II, we did not impose our mores on them; instead, we helped them rebuild. For the most part, Europeans love the U.S.A., except the few socialists who have never experienced our generosity or are too ignorant to understand what we have done for them.

A thought occurred to me the other day why these people meander on the road. At first I thought it was because they want to walk on something smooth, but eventually I realized that it's because their entire life they have had to deal with land mines. Holy cow! Have you ever had to think about that in YOUR life?!?!? There are over six million mines here, thanks to the Russians who did not leave accurate maps of the fields and won't be coming back to clean up their mess. On average, 10 people a day die here as a result of stepping on mines! There is no telling how many are wounded.

Life in Afghanistan is harsh and unforgiving.

CHAPTER 18
HOMESICK

Diggs,

Just thinking about you, my friend. I remember Vietnam being described as hour upon hour of boredom... interrupted by moments of sheer terror. I saw where your camp got rocketed. I don't think that that's an actual word, but I remember using it! I do remember the rockets though. Are your bad guys any better at aiming than our bad guys were? I think that's what made it have a special kind of scary... the hits were random, so staying away from the ammo dump wasn't enough to keep you out of the target area!

We are seeing some protests... 1,000 people in Washington, OOHH! But as much as I want them to get in line behind you proud and brave men, I have to remind myself that the freedom we fight for is for all... not just the ones who think like us.

Michelle and Zoe are in Oklahoma seeing Cheryl's mom for a week. My Lincoln Mark VIII made it to Alaska under the fine steerage of Dusty! Cheryl's brother Paul was very happy to see them both!

I'm glad things are busy here... not being busy can hurt... but I sure need a few days. I shouldn't complain, I'm here in Texas where a fella can have Outback whenever. I'm proud to know ya, Diggs. I'll be mighty happy to see you back, even though I'm too much a pussy to ride the "Milwaukee Iron"! Can't even have a beer with you, but I'll have a near-beer if that'll do!

Keep your head well hidden... perhaps under the dress of a Donut Dolly?

Paul

15 JAN 2003

Dear Friends and Family,

As the moon becomes full and the weekend approaches, we expect rocket attacks. It is the pattern of the attacks—weekends and high illumination. Today is Thursday, and tomorrow with the full moon, 100% illumination will be upon us.

Have I mentioned how beautiful the Afghan nights are? The sky is so clear and the stars so bright. I love to wake up in the morning around 0400 (4:00 a.m.) and just look at the sky for a few minutes—the sky that hasn't changed for thousands of years. In such a place as this, so primitive, it seems surreal. I wish I knew more about the constellations or had a powerful telescope to view the moon and its craters. A few months ago back in the States I attended a conference for people at my bank who hold similar positions to mine and exceeded their goals. The conference sponsors had an astronomy club set up telescopes, and we had the opportunity to view the rings around Saturn and the spot on Jupiter. It was amazing. Even though I was gone for half a year, I think I would have qualified to attend the convention again this year. Guess what? No conventions for the guys fighting the war.

My current location reminds me of Steamboat Springs, Colorado—not at all for the scenery, but for the weather. Our location is much like the base of the mountain. It is cool, yet we can walk about comfortably in light jackets. High mountains covered with snow surround us, and there are actually a dozen or so pine trees close by. Wish I could walk to Double Z's Bar-B-Q in Steamboat Springs right now. Of course, there is always the reality check of having to use an outdoor toilet when it is 20 degrees. Talk about an awakening!

In one way Afghanistan is unlike Colorado; I found a human leg bone near my tent today. The Mujahedeen, when they overran this camp 20 years ago, slaughtered and beheaded 300+ Russian soldiers. They are buried under our compound somewhere. Their heads were placed throughout Bagram and never recovered. The rumor is that my tent is over the burial pit.

I did spend some spare time in the last three days building a humidor out of an ammo can and the wood from three cigar boxes that friends have sent. I now have an airtight, cedar-lined box that will keep everything quite fresh. Other than that, and writing, I've been watching "Band of Brothers" to keep myself occupied in the evenings. The roar of the aircraft taking off and landing nearby makes an early night's sleep quite impossible. Basically, I stay awake until I am exhausted and finally doze off.

We had leftover Outback Steakhouse for dinner tonight. Even cold, old steak is good! I hope to put some weight back on while at Bagram. There is actually a dining facility off the SF compound here that is run by Brown and Root. The food is excellent! They have a spicy cucumber salad that is to die for! I have made several trips over there to eat. I wish I had heard about this sooner! Thank you Halliburton!

I will be going to Paris to visit my sister for a few days at the end of February for a short break/reality check. I can't wait to see her, her husband, and my nephew—and don't forget the new niece! I'm so looking forward not only to seeing them, but to a hot bath and a great glass of champagne. Well, that and an assortment of many other things. It cannot come soon enough. I haven't been this excited about anything since Christmas as a five-year-old.

Along those lines, what do I want when I come home? I want to see my family and friends, eat some quality Mexican food (with quality margaritas, of course), ride my Harley for a few weeks, buy a house, oh...get a job, forgot about that, meet the people who have been writing to me, have my teeth cleaned, take a hot bath, chase the girls a bit, buy new clothes, go hiking in Colorado, ride my mountain bike, swim in a pool, and get a good night's sleep in a real bed. I guess that is about it. Everything else will fall into place. Ya gotta have something to look forward to and dream about at night.

We don't know when we are coming home as of yet. There are many rumors floating around. We could be leaving here anytime after April. I don't know if we are moving on to another destination or not. If any of you are planning to send anything here, do so before the end of February; after that point, hold all mail.

Well, seven pages are enough for the moment. It is very slow at my current location and I do not get out much. The writing will be more interesting once I return to Kabul.

                                        Thanks for the support.
                                        Diggs

CHAPTER 19
BURNS NIGHT SUPPER WITH THE SCOTS

THE CAPTAIN'S LADY
By Robert Burns

O, mount and go,
Mount and make you ready!
O, mount and go,
And be the Captain's Lady.

When the drums do beat,
And the cannons rattle,
Thou shalt sit in state,
And see thy love in battle.

When the vanquish'd foe
Sues for peace and quiet,
To the shades we'll go,
And in love enjoy it.

O, mount and go,
Mount and make you ready!
O, mount and go,
And be the Captain's Lady!

22 JAN 2003

Dear Family and Friends,

I received some exciting news today. The school at Pol-e-charkhi has been chosen as a location for the Army to rebuild! This is all part of the next phase of the war where the U.S. "wins the hearts and minds." In Special Forces this is something we generally initiate right from the beginning; however, the conventional Army takes time before they get to that stage. I was personally invited, through the chaplain, to attend a great feast in honor of the occasion, but due to my current duty I could not make the event. I hear everyone had a wonderful time—lots of music, dancing, and feasting.

There have been so many boxes of supplies and clothing coming in from the U.S. and my friends that it has become almost impossible for us to handle the load. I cannot thank all of you enough for making a difference in the lives of these kids. Just a little bit of hope goes a long way.

This afternoon I found more human bones near my tent. It is impossible to tell how old they are, but I'm willing to bet they have been in the dirt for 10 to 15 years. A skeleton of a Russian soldier, still in uniform, was found not far from here. It is kind of spooky to think about bodies buried in the immediate vicinity—like right under my tent.

25 JAN 2003

I managed to hitch a ride back to my base near Kabul. I was anxious to get in touch with the Scots on the British compound in regard to the annual Burns Night Supper. Robert Burns is a very famous Scottish poet who is revered as the "poet to the common man." His poems that are most recognized by Americans include *Red, Red Rose*, *Tam O'Shanter*, *Auld Lang Syne*, and *To a Mouse*. Believe it or not, there are actually more statues celebrating Burns than William Shakespeare. I brought my kilt to Afghanistan knowing that somewhere there would be Scots and Burns Night celebrated. My hunch paid off.

I met the Scots a few months ago and introduced them to the two pipers we have in our unit. After an introduction and a few cordial visits, we were invited to the supper. This is an honor indeed, as only five outsiders were invited, all resulting from my introductions.

If you ever have the chance to attend a Burns Night Supper, I would recommend taking advantage of the invitation. It is quite an affair with bagpipes, singing, poetry, toasts, and traditional Scottish food, including haggis. Haggis is a mix of oatmeal, sausage, blood, and some other tasty treats, all cooked inside a sheep's stomach. Done right, it is delicious; done wrong, and it's, well, it's haggis.

Sergeant Major Steele of the 51st Highland Regiment wrote a poem for me to read as part of the festivities. I was even listed in the program. What an honor! When the time came, I was introduced by Steele in fine poetic style. I should mention the entire evening is hosted and emceed in poetry. Gathering up my courage, I stood on the table and recited the following in the most dramatic form:

A Yank I am,
But don't ye weep
That I know not
A tattie from a neep,
Nor even a haggis from a sheep!

The highlands through my blood does flow,
The "Famous Grouse" imparts a glow
To face and cheeks, and this I know—
Tonight I'll sleep.

The pipes they squeal,
My soul does feel
For claymore and a fling.
And "Uisge Beatha" – just a dram
Flows down my gullet, and then damn!
I think I actually can sing.

So thank you Robbie for this night,
And thank you President George Bush for the flight
Of fancy to the lands
Of bonnie lassies, whiskey glasses
And bloody feuding clans!

Yes, a Yank I am,
But Scot down deep,
And still don't know
A tattie from a neep.

A standing ovation followed. Not bad for a Yank, huh? The evening was so entertaining, and the presentation was done as formally as any other Burns Nights I have attended. I feel there was special significance due to the fact that we are all soldiers and currently at war.

CHAPTER 20
MORE LETTERS FROM THE CHILDREN

28 JAN 2003

Dear Family and Friends,

Things have been slow here so I thought I would share with you a few letters from the children who are writing me. They are reproduced here completely unedited.

Dear Captan Digs,

My name is Lorrie. I just want to thank you for fighting f or our country. You are so brave for our country you don't even know about. I went to see Santa Clause two last week. You should go see it with your kids. I hope that you are safe and sound. Do you have a sister? I do she's four and her name is Emma. Do you have food? Whats the weather like? It's very cold here. Your so brave to get up every day fight for our country. Are you married? Well, I'm not that's for sure cause I'm only ten. My aunt she has a six year old girl. She wanted an nother one and she found out she is going to have one. She is going to get married soon. In school it is kind of fun but it is also boreing but ha I want to get good grads because I am going to become a dentist. Are you going to stay a soldier? Well if you are good luck!

Your friend, Lorrie

Dear CPT Diggs,

My name is Oscar Daniel Biders I live in Georgia. The Iron Bowl is coming up and I hope the Miami Hurricanes will be their. there was a sniper on the loose in Alabama. It was two of them a 17 year old boy and a old Jamacian man. They were using a M-16 but they were caught. Does it rain a lot in the state you are in? Is there a lot of soldiers with you? What kind of food do you like? Do you fight everyday? I hope you and the rest of the soldiers stay alive and healthy. There was a killing in Alexandria. A teenage boy killed his grandparents for no reason. I cope you come back home safely.

Dear Captain Diggs,

I hear you are real cool so I thought I'd write to you. I am real thankfull for all the good deeds you have done for us. I think you are so brave. When the terrorist attacked I was really afraid, and when I saw tapes and videos about the bombings, I was also sad. Now I don't have to worry about that because you and all the other soldiers are protecting us. I am most thankfull for you trying your best to protet our nation. The wheather is cold around here, and the leaves are beautiful. Now I have some questions to ask. How is the wheather where you are? What kinds os foods do you eat? Have you seen any snakes, scropians, any kinds of bugs?

Hi my name is Shelly Sloan, and Im so glad that you have the strength and courage to go and fight for our country that proves that you car fore out country. And I hope that this war will be over soon so you may go back home to you wife and kids. And about 2 weeks or one week ago this couple this old couple were hurt and killed by his own grandson. It was realy bad thers a lot of killing in this world. But one day I hope their will be piece in all earth people. Im glad you ther right know and I'm sure Jesus Christ will watch over you and keep you in his hand and make sure you never get hurt. And I have faith and hope just like Jesus gave us. And a couple weeks ago it turned realy cold how is it down there? Do you have any pets? Do you tell stories? And do you you are gonna win this war? Course I think you are couse I have fatih and I love you tho I don't know who I am talking to. But I love you.

Dear Captan Digs

I am sad for you & your family. I wish you, others, and my daddy could come back & the war would end. The weather is changing here. The leeves are turning colors. Flags are up everywhere. I hope y have a good Christmas! Thank you for protecting are country. I bet your family misses you. THANK YOU!

Dear Captain Diggs,

God bless you for fighting for our country. My name is Sue Meeker. I am 10 years old, and I just want to cry when I think about you guys in Afghanistan.

The leaves are changing here. The weather is too. It is 10:40 am on a Friday. It is November 8, 2002. How long have you been here in this horrid place? What food do they give you? Do you eat M.R.E.s? There is 3 new movies you need to see. One is called Spiderman, it is not a cartoon. The second is called Eight Legged Freaks. The third one is called Ice Age. It is a cartoon, but it is funnhy. Where is you home in the states? Do you have a family? Where was you born? I was born in Tennessee. Is there any girl soldiers? Do you draw? If you do will you draw me something if you have time? I am a good drawer. Are you a tall man? Sorr I ask questions but I am just curious. How old are you? Wright back please.

Dear Captan,

Thankyou for serving our country. Thanks for fighting for freedom what is it like in Afghanistan it cool to be in America The it very cold here the snipper has beencaught. My Friend thinks wars are fun but he doesn't know the real deal What should I do no be his friend or covince him that wars are not fun When I grow up I am going to serve my contry I know your in gods heart

Dear ~~Cat~~ Captiean Diggs,

I hear its going great over there. I geel great that you are fighting for America in Afghanistan. Well any ways the leaves are changing. They're red, orange, yellow, green, and brown. Our nation is more patrictic now that you have been fighting. I want to wiah you a Happy Thanksgiving and a Merry Christmas. In a few months it will be my birthday on July 10th, 1993. So me and you have something to think about. You have your home and the day you win the war. I have my birthday and the holidays. I can picture what it's like over there but I don't want to say it cause you might not like it to be brung up unless it has to be. I like football baseball and softball. I love the way our country is coming together. I am in the fourth grade. I know you are very busy over there so I will leave you alone.

Dear Captan,

I hope you go home to see your famly. I know how you feel not seeing your family. I have a dad, but he is one of those people who dosen't hardly see his family much. But I stile love him.

3 FEB 2003

Last night we had a helicopter crash that killed four soldiers. This morning we got the news about the Challenger shuttle disaster. There are a lot of people out there sacrificing their lives to keep Americans free and to keep us advancing into the future of mankind. I think President Bush summed it all up in his State of the Union Address when he said:

> The call of history has come to the right country. Americans are a resolute people who have risen to every test of our time. Adversity has revealed the character of our country, to the world and to ourselves.

America is a strong nation and honorable in the use of our strength. We exercise power without conquest, and we sacrifice for the liberty of strangers.

Americans are free people, who know that freedom is the right of every person and the future of every nation. The liberty we prize is not America's gift to the world; it is God's gift to humanity.

We Americans have faith in ourselves, but not in ourselves alone. We do not claim to know all the ways of Providence, yet we can trust them, placing our confidence in the loving God behind all of life and all of history. May he guide us now, and may God continue to bless the United States of America.

Well, I've haven't had a lot to share with you these past few weeks, but hopefully things will pick up a bit when I return to the Kabul area. I am looking forward to taking leave in a couple of weeks, and finally getting a bath and sleeping in a bed.

Keep the faith. We are winning this war.

Cheers!
Diggs

CHAPTER 21
AN AMERICAN IN PARIS

Hi Diggs,

I've been wanting to write you now since last fall and here it is the first week of spring. You don't know me personally, yet I've been hearing about you from my sister, Andrea, since you all first met a good many years ago. Your letters from the front are not only inspiring, but never fail to make my day. By the time I get to your sign off I'm always wiping away the tears.

You'll be glad to know that I've passed your letters on to a few (idiots) who made the mistake of posting (stupid/uninformed) derogatory comments on the President's (as they put it) oppressive regime inside our gov't alongside a few other choice statements about the (then) pending war in Iraq, anti-war rallies directly to people in Romania and Yugoslavia. As I am usually the only hawk in a sea of democrat liberals (due to the nature of my job) I usually keep my opinions to myself, but not this time. My response was short and to the point with an attachment containing your incredible letter about hot loads, the Clintons, every generation's villains and your mission accompanying the 12 year old child inside a steel cased coffin so big for such a little girl, adding 'I dont think Capt Diggs would call what he does serving an oppressive regime! Needless to say, not ONE thing showed up on that bulletin board in 4 days, after that apologies came, and thank yous also for my sharing of your experiences. I guess being a patriot has something to do with having a parent and many relatives in WWII, and being a Navy brat also. I won't ramble on and on as I know you have important things to do where you are.

Just a couple more things before signing off though. Upon your return home to Dallas I would like to extend my services to you whenever you feel the need. This will be my gift to you and just one small way of saying thank you for serving our country in all the ways that you do. Capt Diggs Brown, it's my honor to gift you with two (not one but two) 2-hr sessions of therapeutic massage treatment at your convenience and whenever your schedule permits, of course. I don't expect you to e-mail me back as I know you are busy there. However, after your return U can e-mail me or just get my # from Andrea. Who, by the way, is doing well & cancer free after a double mastectomy over the holidays. This us her first week back on the job full time. Thanx for taking the time to read this, Diggs. I will look forward to finally meeting you after all these years. You are in my prayers each and every morning and evening. Know that all of us who read your letters hold you in our hearts.

> *Sincerely and with affection,*
> *Germaine*

09 MAR 2003

Dear Family and Friends,

No spell check and will be speed typing due to limited access, so bear with me please.

The past few weeks there hasn't been anything that I could really keep record of and relay my experiences to you. The war continues at a steady pace. The attacks on us are random but not few or far between. This is something we have always expected, and with us being "unconventional warriors," our response is measured and calculated. It is like a great game of chess that we are winning.

I did finally get away for a few days to visit my sister and brother-in-law in France. They live about 45 minutes north of Paris in a beautiful medieval village named Senlis. The village was actually a Roman fortress at one time and has walls dating back to the BC times.

At the train station the French police blew up someone's luggage that had been left unattended. They did this without any announcement, and the explosion shook the depot. Everyone jumped, except me. After my arrival at my sister's house, I managed to get a hot bath and a bottle of ice cold champagne to start my holiday. I soaked in the tub for a good hour. Can you imagine?!?! I was able to drink water out of the tap and sleep on a bed! The food was excellent as my brother-in-law is a fantastic cook, and the wines and champagnes were out of this world. I think I probably put back on a few of the pounds I've lost in Big A!

We managed to visit their country home for a few days. It was so nice just to be able to sit on green grass and listen to the birds. I spent a lot of time on the lawn smelling the grass and watching the birds fly through the trees. Needless to say, it was quite a shock to the system to go from barren and cold to lush with peace and quiet. I did find that I was having trouble sleeping because I've been used to hearing jets almost every night.

I managed to do a bit of touring. Some of the typical Parisian tour included the Louvre and Arc de Triomphe. We visited an extraordinary castle a few miles from my sister's home. It's called Chantilly. There is not enough time to go into details of my trip; that will have to be saved for another day, maybe when I get home and over a margarita.

When I left, my sister and nephew stood in their doorway crying as the taxi pulled away. It was tough to leave, but duty calls and one must answer. I had a multitude of thoughts running through my mind as the 8-hour train ride took me back to Germany and closer to the war.

I'm in Germany now, trying to hop a flight back to Afghanistan. Just a couple of more days of civilization and then the hard reality. I will write again as I can and hope to have more of interest in the next letter.

Your support is as always appreciated.

Cheers!
Diggs

CHAPTER 22
REBIRTH OF A NATION

Bon Jour!

How is France? What a place to be now... can you go talk to the powers that be and get them educated on the need to take some action on Iraq? Anyway, I hope you are enjoying your time there. Sounds awesome! Are you going straight from France back home, or do you have to go back to Afghanistan?

Ok, the reason for this e-mail. Have I told you before that just when I think you can't do anything more to amaze me you do???? We got your box today. I just stood there in awe at your generosity!!! The kids couldn't believe a soldier who is as busy as you are would think of them like this. They LOVED the scarves and hats!!! They cannot wait to meet you. I think you have yourself a fan club forming. Of course I am president! Seriously Diggs, thank you sooo much for not only sending all of it, but for the thought of it as well. I love the ring too. It gets a lot of attention, and I get excited to say it is from Afghanistan!

I heard that a few of our boxes finally made it there to Afghanistan. There are some Christmas presents in those boxes for you. I wonder if you'll get them??? The kids also made some posters for you and your students. There are some pictures of the kids, too, to share with the students. I am crazy that the shipment didn't get there sooner. Oh well, it will all work out. I think in all there were about 40 large boxes, and about 10 or so smaller ones.

We go on break starting next week for 3 weeks. We come back on the last week of March, and then we only have 9 weeks of school left. I hope you can make it out to see the kids. I am telling you, they have a million questions for you, and are just dying to meet you. Remember to that you are having dinner with me one night when you get back. I want to hear all your stories.

I am glad you are on the final lap of your tour. Get home soon, and be safe!!!

Thank you a million times over again for all that you've done. You are still a Rock Star in my book!!!

> *ooxxooxx*
> *Michelle*

12 MAR 2003

Dear Family and Friends,

I have to admit that toward the end of my 10-day leave in France, I was anxious to get back to Kabul and the rest of my unit. It wasn't guilt (most of the soldiers have taken some sort of pass or leave) but a sense of duty. Those of you who have worked with me in the civilian world know that I never leave a job unfinished. When I got back to our base there were many soldiers I hadn't seen in over eight weeks. Everyone had a joyful "Welcome back" on their lips and also, "When are you going to reopen the Fabulous Bombay Lounge?" It is nice to know you are missed.

Afghanistan seems to me to have gone through a transformation in the past few weeks; it is almost like a rebirth. The days have warmed up to a pleasant 50° to 70°, although the nights still get down to freezing, and the skies are clear. There are patches of green sprouting up all around—and in places I never would have imagined. If you recall, I came into Afghanistan early last September after the hot, dry Afghan summer and five years of drought. At that point there wasn't anything green, only dirt and dead vegetation. The winter snow has brought life to the dry plains.

The mighty Kabul River is flowing and it is a good sign. (The actual river is not as impressive as its name may suggest.) The snowcaps are beginning to recede, allowing irrigation to begin. The locals tell me this is the most precipitation they have had in years, and they believe the Americans brought the rain when they chased out the Taliban. Farmers are plowing their fields using antiquated tractors, mules, and manpower. I have seen a great many men using shovels to dig out irrigation ditches. The flocks of sheep and goats are growing daily as the newborn ewes make their appearance. The herds are everywhere, and the nomads are beginning their migration back to the northern pastures.

A nomadic family on the move. Everything they own is packed on the donkeys and camels. These families can move up to 20 miles in a day.

The rebirth is also prevalent in the spirit of the people. There is so much construction going on. The focus is not only on rebuilding, however, but beautification as well. I have been told that the area we are in used to be heavily forested, but the Russians destroyed the vegetation because the Mujahedeen would use the trees for cover when they attacked. People are planting trees once again. Homes are being gaily painted and tiled. Even our camp is starting to take on a civilized look with a new dining area recently completed (to include paint and lights), and the exteriors of our buildings are being touched up. Several new gas stations are being built along the Jalalabad Road, which is the main highway through Kabul. While primitive, this is a sign that there is a demand for fuel, which means people have money to spend and businesses are growing. Something of interest, the gas stations have neon lights—1950's style, cool!

Even the dreaded burka is on the endangered species list. I have noticed more women wearing just veils or scarves, and a few are not covering their faces at all. Still nothing showing above the ankle, but at least they can now see the light of day. I even saw a woman driving! What is the world coming to? We continue to hear from the locals about how glad they are that we are here and their hopes that the American soldiers do not leave soon. It will be interesting to see what happens when Iraq kicks off. I wouldn't expect much trouble from the locals.

12 MAR 2003

As I awaited transportation to Kabul, I had the opportunity to meet Geraldo Rivera. He is a petite man with a huge ego and pink sunglasses. I am not very impressed with him, although our brief conversation was amicable. I can understand how some might think he is a great guy. I asked him if he wants to come to our base and see what is really going on, but he declined.

13 MAR 2003

Chaplain Andy made another trip to the local orphanage to deliver clothing and school donations received from the U.S.A. Many of these donations came from those of you who read my e-mails. So far we have received over two tons of clothing and school supplies, and we've had well over $3,000 donated! Again, I can't thank you enough. Your thoughtfulness has been making a difference to these very poor people. In a couple of days I plan on going out to our school at Pol-e-charki to hand out the school supplies you have donated. School is getting a late start this year due to the construction that has also been supported by you, the folks at home, and most recently, the U.S. Army.

16 MAR 2003

The war with Iraq looks like it will start soon. If so, this will be a very interesting time that we all live in. I don't expect it to end as rapidly as the first "Desert Storm." I believe there is much more at stake in this war. The Muslim world will be watching to see just how much resolve we have as a nation. Our lack of response to the first attacks on the World Trade Tower, the USS Cole, and our embassies have given our enemies the impression that we are complacent and can be bullied.

18 MAR 2003

Today I had the opportunity to take supplies to one of our firebases in the middle of nowhere. The scenery reminded me very much of the Colorado high plains with snowcapped mountains and sparse vegetation. The mountains, of course, are of higher elevations than Colorado and very stark in their appearance.

The road we took was in poor condition, although it is considered a major thoroughfare. It was blacktop, two lanes, and full of potholes. The road winded though many villages where the people were happy to see us. It seems that their entertainment is watching the road for strangers passing through. Almost everyone waves and the kids give the thumbs up and call out, "Thank you!" I've often wondered where the Afghanis learned the thumbs up and English?

Caravans of nomads are moving and we passed many of various sizes. Entire clans are moving on horseback, camelback, and walking with their herds of sheep, camels, and goats. I got some great photos—well, as good as you can get in a moving vehicle. These nomads must move miles every day to stay ahead of the weather and keep up with the pastures as they begin to green. They must also pass through the villages and put up with the traffic. Several times we must stop for a herder to get his sheep and goats out of our path.

The day was overcast and as we gained elevation, a light snow began to fall. Our journey took us through a winding and steep mountain pass much more treacherous and higher than any I have encountered in Colorado. The pass itself had large fallen boulders strewn across it making the drive that much more tense. At the higher elevations there was plenty of snow pack, and the temperatures were definitely below freezing. Imagine, if you can, walking through this with your herd of sheep!

We spent a few hours at the firebase conversing with our friends and dropping off supplies. They are in good spirits considering the quality of life they must endure to be out here in the great void.

The rain became heavy, and it was time to return to Kabul. The drive was slow in the blinding snow that was mixed with heavy rain. Again we passed herds of sheep on the move, but for the most part the nomads have pitched their tents to get out of the weather. Their camels and donkeys brave the cold and snow. Inside, the tents must be warm with their stoves and wool rugs used not only for flooring but also to insulate the walls. It must be a very difficult life at times, and yet when it is spring, summer, and early fall, what a pleasure to live under the stars.

20 MAR 2003

The war with Iraq has begun. I'm hoping that Saddam has been taken out with an immediate missile strike, but am sure it will be days before we find out. Keep the boys over there in your prayers.

On this day, Chaplain Andy and I, along with a security force, went to the school at Pol-e-charki to distribute the school supplies that many of you have sent. I was pleasantly surprised to see the renovations that have occurred at the school. There is now a 5-foot-tall stone wall surrounding the compound. Toilets (outdoor and outhouse type) have been built. There is glass in every window and wood-burning heaters in each room. The walls have been patched and painted a light shade of yellow, and each room has either a black or white board. School desks are just starting to come in now, and hopefully, the project will be complete in a very few days. Of course, Taliban and al Qaeda are offering large sums of money to anyone who will destroy the school.

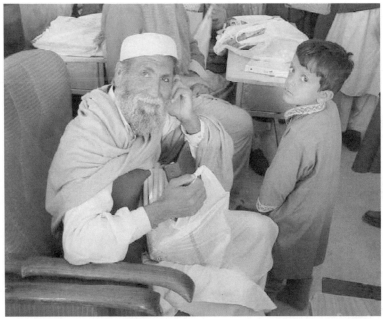

The school donations from home built a bridge of friendship with all generations of Afghanis.

We got a late start on our movement to the school, so by the time we got there, all the teachers were patiently waiting for us in a classroom. Since I had not been there in quite awhile, I saw a lot of new faces, but the old hands still knew me and welcomed me back. We moved a large amount of supplies into one room. These are to be the initial issue to get classes started. Chaplain Andy gave a short speech in regard to the school being refurbished and how the supplies were sent from all of you back home—not the U.S. government. The teachers were impressed by this and wanted to make sure that you received thanks. After the speech, we gave each teacher a bag to fill with what was needed to get them started for the school year. There will be more supplies distributed later because we have more than enough to support this school for at least one semester. I thought it was interesting that the female teachers did not cover their faces and were not shy. They are educated and so far ahead of their peers in knowledge and self-determination.

In a few days Andy and I are to return to Pol-e-charki to a feast and celebration. The Afghanis are without a doubt the most grateful people I have met in all my travels. I would love to return here in five years or so and see the progress that has been made.

21 MAR 2003

Once a month we hold a large bazaar at the main gate, in addition to those we hold on Fridays. Today is the monthly bazaar. I'm well known among the merchants because I give their children toothbrushes, toothpaste, and occasionally candy. There is a cute little boy who must be four years old who recognizes me and always wanders over to me to wave. To the merchants I am "Brown" or "my good friend." It is not uncommon to have several of them ask me to sit and share tea with them. My favorite merchant is Hamid. He owns three rug shops in Kabul and is a regular at our bazaar. He speaks English, Russian, and French. I spent over four hours today with him sitting on rugs and sipping hot tea under the glaring sun. Today we discussed, at great length, life under the Taliban. The stories he told would make your hair stand on end; everything from beatings for not having a long enough beard, to walls being pushed on top of women who have premarital sex, to mass executions in the stadium. There is no one in their right mind who wishes the return of the Taliban! He told me also that the Afghanis are not upset about the Iraq liberation. He believes that the majority of Middle Easterners know Saddam is an evil man who must be removed from power. I believe this to be true, also.

I guess I'd better get this mail out now so that you know I am safe and sound here. I hope to return home soon.

Keep our soldiers and President in your prayers, and boycott French products. ☺

Cheers!

Diggs

My friend, Hamid, and his cousin, Atta, sit among their rugs. Hamid is a brilliant entrepreneur and a very educated man. His business was always brisk at our weekly bazaar.

CHAPTER 23
WRAPPING THINGS UP

Cpt. Diggs,

I am the mom of a third grader in Mrs. Street's class at Meeker Elementary, Greeley, CO. Sgt. Blum is a friend of mine who had been e-mailing your absolutely amazing letters to me. I began to e-mail them to Mrs. Street and then it all took off from there. Troy has gone in several times and seen the class. Personally I feel that entire experience has been one that the whole class has been lucky to have. My little girl, Haley, will never forget this and I hope it shapes and strengthens her patriotism and pride in being an American. I am truly sorry to hear about your uncle. It sounds like you have a great group of guys there. I was privy enough a couple years ago to spend a week in San Diego, witnessing the metamorphous that the Marine corps calls boot camp. My father served in the Navy during the tail end of the Korean War and I was red, white and blue way before 9-11. You are very much a hero among heroes. I hope that time allows for you to come and visit Meeker when you return home. I'm still envious of the great deal you got on your Harley.

There is nothing like the freedom of the open road. I can appreciate that . I'm Harleyless at the moment, had to spend what little I had saved on a 3500 mile road trip last summer. Was a great trip. If it had been on a Harley it would have been better. hahahahahahahaha.

I have started a couple letters before to write you and thank you, but they either got erased or lost, something about my mailbox being too full to send anything. I did not want to miss a chance to say thank you and that I hope you find your way back to Meeker. We would all love to meet you and see the famous Cpt. Diggs in person. God bless you and keep you safe.

Sincerely,

Holly K Cronk

It would be very difficult to find anyone more giving than the American soldiers and citizens. This day we delivered to an orphanage over one ton of supplies donated by you back home.

23 MAR 2003

Dear Family and Friends,

There have been many world-shaping events in the past few days. The war has begun with Iraq. It has been discovered that the Russians have been selling military equipment to the Iraqis in violation of the UN sanctions. The French also have been dealing with Saddam, mostly with illegal oil shipments, and we wonder why they didn't want to be part of the coalition. Just wait and see what other revelations will come out after Iraq falls. I tend to wonder if delegates in the UN have also had illegal dealings with the Iraqis? Who has been lining their pockets with the "food for oil" program? Why are they so concerned over intervening in Iraq, a country that has thumbed its collective nose at the UN for a decade?

Today Chaplain Andy, several soldiers from the MPs, and I went to the local orphanage, Allahuddin, to hand out food and clothing that you folks back home have sent. The area of town where the orphanage is located is devastated. Entire city blocks have been wiped out by years of war; and yet, some people still inhabit these ruins. Our caravan consisted of one armored Hummer in lead, an SUV carrying the chaplain, myself, and three others, a large cargo truck, and another armored Hummer pulling up the rear.

When we pulled up to the gate we were greeted by the headmaster of the orphanage and some of his staff. This is our fourth trip to deliver the goods, and with every trip the tone becomes more cordial. It is obvious the children know that the Americans are helping them, and they all do their best to speak English. Some will give us the same sentence over and over again because those are the only words they know. Typical is, "Hello, how are you?"

After taking 20 minutes or so to stack cans of vegetables and pallets of clothing, we were given a tour of the facility. In this particular orphanage there are just under 1,000 children ranging from newborn to 18 years old. At 18 they are turned out to the street, but not empty handed; they have an education and a learned trade to get them started. The children we meet are so much better behaved than the children we meet out on the street. Part of their curriculum must be manners. I made it a point to bring a large bag of candy with me that I handed out to the children and the supervisors as I met them. Some of the children have learned to make rugs, and their hands are stained with the natural dyes they produce from the flower petals. A high-quality rug will take approximately one year to make.

Once again our trip to the orphanage was a success. We said our goodbyes, knowing that this will be our last trip. The headmaster was very sad to see us go. He had a group of young girls come over and sing us a couple of native songs as a gesture of thanks. Two little boys, not older than 10, then had a singing competition, each one singing a few verses as loudly as possible. This was all very entertaining. The commander of the new military police company on our compound made today's trip with us, and she swears that she will follow in our footsteps.

27 MAR 2003

Today we graduated another battalion of Afghan soldiers, this being our eighth to train. I was in charge of making all of the arrangements for the ceremony, as well as handling the numerous VIPs who attended. There were over 700 students; not a bad class size, I might add.

This ceremony turned out to be less elaborate than those in the past, and the simplicity of it made it that much more enjoyable for all concerned. Part of the ceremony included the soldiers taking an oath to Afghanistan, to the government of Afghanistan, and to Allah. They were marched to a very long table that had Korans spaced out the length of the table. Each soldier placed his right hand on the Koran as he repeated the pledge.

It was an uplifting moment for all of the American soldiers involved in training this group of men. They have taken individuals from the different tribes of Afghanistan and, despite their initial differences, molded them into a cohesive battalion. Men who could not march or shoot, and some unable to read or write, are now professional soldiers with a career of which they can be proud. Of course, there is still a long way to go, but the transition, simply put, is outstanding.

Today there was also a "thank you" celebration for Chaplain Andy and me at Pol-e-charkhi School. I was late getting there because I was coordinating the graduation of the Afghan army battalion. By the time I showed up, the feast was over, but I did have the chance to say goodbye to the teachers and some of the students. For me it was a very moving moment. We have seen this school come from a ruin to almost completely restored. Again, much of the restoration is the result of your contributions. The staff wanted to make sure that I thanked you for the support. Chaplain Andy has done a fine job in making everything work out.

An interesting note: If you remember when I first started assisting in teaching English at this school I sent a photo home of a young girl watching the class through the window. She is a very shy and quiet child. Today she wanted to sit with me. She finally spoke to me and said, "Thank you." I've enclosed that photo. Something else to notice in the photo is that there is now glass in the windows, desks, and paint in the room. The electricity is going to be running in another week or so. Each room has a black or white board. Amazing what a little compassion can do in making a huge difference in another human's life.

Farista, the shy little girl, finally sits beside me to say goodbye. Note that the teachers in the background are not wearing burkas.

It is raining again. An electrical storm has blown in and the winds have really picked up. We have had more rain this year than in the last seven combined. Our compound has been flooding because we are the low spot between mountains. We are naming the new lake (that once was our road through camp) "Lake Porkchop" after the deceased camp dog that I mentioned earlier.

28 MAR 2003

Today was our weekly bazaar. I made the effort to go down and see my friends, the merchants. It is a wet, dreary day and a bit on the cool side, but they are all there eager to make a buck or two. I think I have bought pretty much all there is to buy and should just open my own shop. My rug dealer friends are jokingly telling all the soldiers that I'm now the merchant and they have to deal with me. I think I made them some serious money today, selling five rugs. The only items I bought today are camel saddlebags and two small silk door decorations that Bedouins hang at their tent entrances. Just what I needed!

One of my favorite interpreters invited me to dine with his family today. Tem lives near downtown Kabul with his mother, father, two brothers, one sister, and aunt. Tem's father is a physician and his mother is a school teacher. This was my first time to visit this part of town, an area that is considered upper middle class.

Chaplain Andy and two other soldiers came with me, and as we drove into the neighborhood, Tem was waiting for us at the street so that he could guide us back to a parking area near his home. As we turned off the main street, the road was no more than a muddy quagmire. The parking area was full of mud and deep puddles. Good thing we were wearing boots with our civilian clothing. We had to navigate two mud roads to get to Tem's home. The roads have a sewage drain dug down the middle, very much as things have been for centuries over here. You really don't want to look too closely at the drain because everything (literally everything) is there. These homes do not have toilets as we know them, but simple drop holes that lead to the drain in the street. Arrgh! Trash has been tossed out of windows on occasion to also be washed down the street. It was a slippery walk up to Tem's house.

The homes here are mud brick. Tem's family lives in the second story of one of these structures. We climbed a tightly turning staircase to reach his foyer. Here we removed our shoes and stepped inside. The living room is probably 12' x 12' with two large rugs covering the floor and cushions on the floor lining each wall for seats. The walls are painted a pale blue, and the rooms of the home are separated by wool blankets draped in the doorways.

There was a nearby mosque, its loudspeaker just outside the window—or so it seemed. Just as we were about to make our introductions, the loud speaker blasted to life announcing noon prayer. It took roughly 10 minutes for the call to prayer and then another 10 minutes for services. During this time our conversation was strained, to say the least. In case you didn't know, the Muslims pray at 5:00 in the morning (they wake me up every day with the loud speaker near our camp), noon, 6:00-ish in the evening, and then around 9:00 at night. In fact, I can hear a prayer as I'm typing this tonight.

Tem's father is a well educated man and speaks a bit of English. He is also a gracious host. We were given hot tea to sip as the conversation began. When it was time for lunch, Tem's younger brother brought in a plastic tablecloth and spread it on the floor in front of each of us as we sat cross-legged. The youngest brother then came by with a kettle of hot water and a bowl. He poured the water over our hands so that we could wash before dining. The little sister followed her brother with a towel for us to dry our hands.

The brother then brought in lunch. It consisted of a bottle of Zam Zam (a cola drink) and a bottle of orange soda. We were given a glass of each. Afghan bread is oblong and flat, about 20 inches in length and 8 inches wide. It has wonderful flavor, especially when it is served hot, as it was then. The bread can be used as a plate, which can then be eaten. How is that for easy cleanup? Along with the bread, we were given a bowl of soup that consisted of lamb and a tomato base. The Afghanis love chips (fries), and a bowl was set out in front of each of us. There were also two large plates of sliced radishes, green onions, sliced tomatoes, basil, and mint. I was in heaven. The bread is torn into pieces and used to line the bowl to soak up the broth. The plates of chips and vegetables are common plates that everyone picks off of. As we dined, it was just the men. The women dined in a separate area, and at that point I had yet to meet them.

When the meal was finished, we went through the same hand-washing ritual again. Once the tablecloth was folded up, Tem's mother and aunt came into the room. This is a rare occasion in Afghanistan. As a rule, the women never mingle with the men, especially strangers. However, Tem's family is educated and more progressive than many. His mother and aunt did not have their faces covered. (I am going to throw in here that Tem's aunt is stunning. She must be in her mid-20s and is just beautiful, with dark eyes and hair.)

We had a short conversation with Tem's family, with him doing a lot of translating. I let his parents know how much I've enjoyed having Tem work for me and what a great time I have had in their country. They were flattered and let me know that Tem had told them a lot about me. They have been anxious to meet me for many months. Apparently, the custom here is to give your guests gifts, and we each received a scarf. I gave Tem's family an expensive box of chocolate that I purchased in the Italian PX.

Before we could carry on much more conversation, our time was up because I had to be back at the base to meet with a German general. We said our goodbyes with Tem's father, shaking our hands with two hands and, as is the custom, touching cheeks. As we shook hands he said to us, "Do not forget us." Wow!

We donned our body armor and departed. The rains had started once again.

Cheers,
Diggs

CHAPTER 24
HOMEWARD BOUND

Diggs,
   I wish you a safe and speedy trip home. I would like to invite you to visit our school once you get home and settled in. Our last day of school is around May 20th. We understand that you will be overwhelmed when you get back with everyone's request for your visit; however, our 1st grade teachers are starting to plan for your visit. They are so excited.

Take care,
Marsha :-)

30 MAR 2003

I've finished packing most of my heavy gear, leaving just some traveling clothes and toiletries in a light bag for the long trip home. Today the customs department will come by and check the pallets for any violations of the codes. When they have finished, our pallets will be moved to the airfield for staging.

The first airlift is out tomorrow. Our replacements, active duty Special Forces, have come in and there are a lot of soldiers looking for a spot to call their own. My bed is the hot item. Several soldiers have come up and want to place dibs on it. If you recall, I built a grand bed that is suspended off the floor allowing for more storage space. Can I even recall how many nights I spent freezing in that room? Not a worry now, the weather has turned beautiful; however, it will be extremely hot here in just a matter of a few weeks. Glad I won't be around for it.

I made it over to see the interpreters and said my last goodbyes. Out of the 30 "terps" we have, I have used two extensively, Tem and Mahboobla. Of course, they want to come to America and I wish they could, but they are destined to stay here and rebuild their country.

I had a quiet night in the medical quarters smoking a fat stogie and swapping stories with the docs. They are such a great group of guys. They have impressed me with their compassion for the people of this country. We had a bit of reminiscing and a lot of laughs throughout the evening.

01 APR 2003

Dear Family and Friends,

It is hard for me to believe that my tour is almost over. The past seven months in Afghanistan have flown by. Our camp seems so empty. It is an emotional time as I sit here typing this letter to you. How can I put into words everything that is going through my head? It is not easy.

I left my career in Colorado to "liberate the oppressed," as our Special Forces creed states. In doing so, my life has become richer, and I am much more appreciative of the things that we Americans take for granted. I feel almost enlightened in regard to the workings of our civilization and our place in the universe. My perspective of my life and the lives of the people I know has gone through some serious changes.

As a member of the National Guard it has been my obligation, duty, and honor to serve my country and defend her citizens. This I know we have done well. Our years of training prepared us for this mission, and we accomplished the tasks at hand in proud manner. No one dislikes war more than the soldier, for he is the one who must sacrifice. With that in mind, I cannot think of one soldier here who has complained in regard to our mission and the fact that we are thousands of miles from our homes and loved ones. We have been willing to pay the price and willing to make that ultimate sacrifice for God and country.

I have met so many good soldiers here—top quality people. I have new friends from several countries, and I hope that they will come to visit me someday, as I hope to visit them again. I have learned who can be trusted and counted on, both here and at home. I have also met people here that I could care less if I ever see again. I have watched people buckle under pressure while others succeeded. The flaws and virtues of mankind have become much clearer in my eyes.

I know for a fact that our presence here has made a difference in the lives of the Afghanis, not only by our mission-driven tasks, but the additional civic duties we accomplished. Although it has been seven months, it seems like just a few days ago when Chaplain Andy and I walked into a bombed-out, broken schoolhouse and asked if we could teach English to the children. That schoolhouse is almost completely restored at this time, thanks to you and your fellow citizens. Our medical teams have saved literally over a thousand lives by providing medications and treatment. Doc Enz has corrected so many crossed eyes I have lost count. The list could go on and on because these events were repeated many times by other American soldiers across this country. Wars are not won only by the battle; you must also "win the hearts and minds" of the populace.

We have brought stability to a country that has not seen peace in over 30 years. We have brought education to an illiterate society. We have given the Afghanis freedom of choice in their lives. The children are eating proper meals, going to school, and wearing clothes that will keep them warm and shoes to protect their feet. They are the living testimony to the fact that Americans are the most generous and caring people on the planet. The United States of America is the last refuge on this earth for human liberty. Be proud to be an American, be proud of your president, and be proud that you have supported a just and noble cause.

America's self-determined liberty has made us the strongest nation in history, both spiritually and materially. We must not make the same mistake of surrendering our heritage as have the Europeans (in particular the French), Africans, and Asians; this will only lead us to ruin. We are one of the youngest countries on the planet, yet the oldest democracy. Our society was founded squarely on the concept of human liberty and continues to exist because we are willing to defend the rights of the individual, both at home and abroad.

There are those who say that when America wages a war, we create more enemies in the Muslim world. There will always be fanatics who hate America and what we stand for. They will always want to destroy our country and way of life, no matter what the circumstance. The Middle Eastern region of the world is scattered with religious infidels who have forgotten the words of Muhammad, "Let none of you treat his brother in a way he himself would dislike being treated." These people have no concept of what some Americans take for granted—our freedom. Corrupt religious fanatics, along with those who are greedy for power and oil money, control the lives of millions of Muslims.

We are dealing with countries that have not yet emerged out of the Dark Ages—countries with the desire to acquire weapons of mass destruction, if not already in their possession. You are the target. The cruelty of the Taliban is beyond your imagination. The same goes for Saddam. The majority of the Iraqi people will rejoice when that war ends and Saddam is removed from power.

Once again the Americans have come as liberators, not conquerors. I can tell you that the greater part of the Afghan population loves us and loves our country. We have done so much for them; we have given them their sovereignty.

I know that all of the soldiers here face the uncertainty of what is in store for us when we return home. How have our families changed and, in some cases, grown? Two of the guys' wives had babies while we were away. There have been changes on both sides of the ocean. Wives have had to take on responsibilities they might not have had to deal with in the past. My hope is that their husbands accept the changes and move smoothly back into their roles.

I'm hoping to return to my position at the bank and pick up where I left off, but will that happen? At this point I can only guess. There are so many difficult decisions and factors determining how we will be received. It is up to you, the family members, employers, and neighbors to welcome home the troops and bring them back into the fold.

02 APR 2003

One day and a wake-up! As my friend Paul would say, "I'm so short I can walk under a snake while wearing a top hat." Our final baggage has been inspected, and we are free for the rest of the day.

The first bus of men heading home today passed us on the parade field, and we gave them the thumbs up and our best "How are you?" mimicking the Afghan children. This was good chuckle for everyone. You could see the excitement in the faces of the guys as they passed by and turned out of the gate.

Several of the troops and I climbed to the roof of one of the two-story buildings to get some sun on our winter-white bones. Everyone was discussing some part of the mission that is a fond or not so fond memory.

Today was strictly a day to relax and watch the world go by. Several goat herds were moving down the Jalalabad Road, with drivers weaving in and out to avoid mutton for lunch. The horns of the trucks, which here are very distinct, sounded every few minutes. Afghan soldiers trained in the background. The new recruits are learning to march.

From over the horizon came the first C-17 transport carrying our guys home. We gave it a cheer as it passed low overhead. It made a steep banking turn and, in a matter of moments, was out of sight. Did the guys cheer when it went wheels up off the runway? I'll bet they did.

After getting thoroughly sunburned, I made it down to the recently completed patio that stands where the once Fabulous Bombay Lounge made its début. I'm not ready to sit inside at this point, the day is just too fine. Hauling out a table and chairs, I am the first to use the new patio in any capacity. Soon a crowd gathers. Everyone stops by to observe the backgammon game that is taking place. I'm wearing my Bombay Lounge baseball cap. It has become a hit with the new guys, and I tell them the saga of the lounge. Who knows, maybe the lounge will remain open here when I return home.

Our camp is eerily quiet as it has been all day. We've turned in our weapons, destroyed whatever paperwork needed to be destroyed, and have erased the hard drives of our working computers. There is nothing left to do now but wait. I can't believe that this is my last night in Afghanistan. The mullah is calling a prayer in the distance. The stars are coming out. The electric generators are humming in the background. This is it, time to move on.

03 APR 2003

I could hardly sleep last night! Today is the day! We are preparing to board the bus that will take us to the airfield. You can feel the excitement in the air. Many of the guys are having their last photos made on our compound with the Afghan flag flying in the background. Our Afghan soldiers are hurriedly going about their business as their training day begins. They pass us at a dead run back to their training area after they draw their weapons from the arms room. Occasionally one will yell something in our direction as they go by. The interpreter tells us they are wishing us a safe journey home.

It is time to leave; we board the bus. Everyone is talkative and anxious for the journey to begin. There is a last chance to say goodbye to our friends, so several take advantage of it. The bus starts up and we are on our way. As soon as we exit the front gate of our compound, an eerie silence befalls the bus. One and all are deep in thought. We have been on this road many times before, so many times that some of the children who greet us are recognized. I believe that a few of them know we are leaving; you can see it in their faces as they give the last thumbs up and wave as we pass. Well, they will have a new group of American soldiers to become acquainted with.

I remember arriving in Afghanistan on this same road at daybreak seven months ago. The people were just beginning to stir. It all seemed so surreal at the time. It was as if we had stepped into a time machine and set the dial for 1700 AD. My mindset was that this has to be one of the poorest countries I have visited, and I have traveled to many. Now I can see change. Is it just that my eyes have been opened by this experience, or is there really a society rebuilding right before my eyes in such a short time? I think both.

We arrive at the airfield. Time passes, seeming like an eternity, and then suddenly in the distance our freedom bird appears as just a small dot. Within minutes it roars past us on the tarmac, tires smoking as the brakes are applied. This monster of an aircraft taxis up to our location and shuts down its engines. The tailgate opens to reveal the cavernous belly. Our equipment is loaded, and I am amazed at just how much this aircraft can hold. We take our seats and strap in. The engines roar to life one by one. Since there are no windows on the aircraft for passengers, my last glimpse at Afghanistan is out the closing tailgate, and then it is gone. I feel like I've aged a lifetime.

Will I return to this country in the future? I doubt if I will, but then you can never bet against it, either. I can imagine that 10 or so years from now one wouldn't recognize the Afghanistan of today. I hope that is true, for their sake.

04 APR 2003

We spent the past 30 hours flying, not including layovers for refueling, and we passed through 12 time zones. In all of this travel we lost a day. We are looking a bit haggard with wrinkled clothing and five o'clock shadows, but our spirits are high.

Our first stop stateside in Maine was greeted by one of the guy's parents and sister who brought fresh baked brownies and cookies. Air Force reservists who are now on active duty were at this location. They were in awe, as we were the first war veterans to pass through their station. They gave us a warm welcome home that was greatly appreciated. Even more prized was flushing toilets and hot water in a porcelain sink to wash our hands at the airfield.

06 APR 2003

Home at last! Colorado never looked so good! We were warned before we returned that there were major changes to expect. Among them are sky-high gasoline prices and peace demonstrations reminiscent of the Vietnam era.

So far I haven't seen any peace demonstrations, but on the other hand, I have had many people come up to me and thank me (and the other soldiers, of course) for protecting the country. Perhaps that is because Colorado Springs is a military town. I would like to think that the majority of U.S. citizens appreciate the sacrifice that their service members are making—sometimes the ultimate sacrifice.

We are home for a couple of months while the decision is made whether we are going back out to war or will be home for good. I can't say which way it appears we are headed.

For the moment, my sojourn is complete.

> Cheers!
> Diggs

CHAPTER 25
HOME AT LAST!

Welcome Home, Diggs!
I'm so glad you're safely stateside...We've been anxiously waiting for just this message.

Yes, many of us are deeply humbled by the work you and your comrades have completed in Afghanistan; the military work and the civilian/humanitarian missions you've completed.

Because of you and men like you, my students, friends and I see the war from a specific perspective; one of personal clarity and realistic objectivity. I wish more Americans had the opportunity to have an inside the war contact like yourself. Perhaps if more did, the protestors and fanatics (on both sides of religious fanaticism) would see the human problems associated with war and peace, not just the political/religious issues.

I'm smiling at the end of a long Sunday. Thank you, thank you for sharing your odyssey with me and my students, our family and friends. I agree; you should seek out a scriptwriter and publish or make this into a movie. It has all the elements of drama—one of the better war movie plots I've seen in a long time.

Please rest, eat, sleep, party; take good care of yourself now that you're stateside.

We want to see you when you're able. I hope you can stay home (U.S.) for awhile, before you have to go back to work—here or abroad.

I'm thankful you're home. I'm thankful for men and women like you.

> *God bless.*
> *Cheryl*

Cheers to you, Diggs!!!
As I read the last few days of your Afghan experience, I began to weep.....I feel like in one small week I could see how you could

find it sad to leave. It must be hard to do so much for a country and its people and then leave that. You are an amazing man and you must know that you have changed lives forever.....you have touched strangers....myself included, with your kindness and generosity. I know how proud of you I am, but America is proud to have you as a citizen, soldier, and patriot. You are a shinning example of all that is good. Welcome home......thank you sooooo much for your sacrifice and courage. I trust we can keep in touch.....and if you are ever in LA....you had better look me up. Thank you again for everything you've done....welcome home!

xoxox
Karri

PS...if you haven't already heard Darryl Worley's new song "Have You Forgotten"...you have to get it...it's a single. He wrote it based on his trip.

Dear Diggs,
  I hope you don't mind receiving an e-mail from a total stranger, but your friend David sent your last two messages to all of us in his office and I just wanted to let you know how much I enjoyed your descriptions of the people and the country of Afghanistan.
  I'm happy that you are home, grateful for the work that you have done and wanted to thank you for representing our great country so well.

May God bless you and your family!
Mary

Welcome home soldier!!
  Well, things just have not been the same around here without you. We all miss you so much, at least those of us who are left. I am sure you have heard about the new round of changes we are trying to survive through. All of the new people who have come on

to our team are anxious to meet you for they have heard so much about you. We all looked forward to the e-mails Jeri would forward on to us letting us know how you were doing. It was amazing to think what kind of world you were living in and the missions you were completing. Thank you for everything you have done to try and help another culture and what you have done to help protect your fellow citizens. I admire you for your courage and strength, your ability to put others ahead of yourself, and most of all to do it with such resilience. You are a hero in my book.

I have a friend who is in the Air Force. He is stationed in Florida. I hope you don't mind but I have been sending him your correspondence that Jeri forwarded to us. His goal is to be in the Special Forces. He has his enrollment package to begin training but with everything going on it has been hard for him to collect the signatures he needs. The first time I sent him a few letters he called me and said, "I don't think you have any idea the magnitude of what your friend does." He went on to say that you are doing exactly what he would like to do with his military career. He was envious and full of admiration for you. If you two are both in Colorado at the same time I will have to introduce you.

So when are you coming up to Fort Collins? We can't wait to see you, so make it soon.

Miss You,
Christine

Dear Diggs,

God love you, honey, I'm so glad to hear that you're back! David called me this afternoon to see if I had gotten your letter, and as I never gave you my home computer address, I didn't know. So he forwarded it to me.

I can't tell you how thrilled I am that your tour is complete (for now, at least) and that you're making your re-assimilation into "regular" society. I cannot sufficiently express my pride in what you and our troops did/are doing...and the selflessness with which you do it.

Thank God for your safe return and the incredible experience that only added greater beauty, depth and soul to the wonderful, loving man you have always been.

Perhaps some day or paths will cross again...if you make a visit to Dallas, I just might have to fly in for that.

I love you, Diggs, and am proud to know you and call you my friend.

With love and respect,
Di

08 MAY 2003

Dear Friends and Family,

I debated writing anything further since my return from Afghanistan. Comparatively speaking, events in my life have slowed to such a point that they appear to teeter on the edge of sheer boredom and may be of little interest to anyone. This perception changed last night when I met with some of my friends from the bank in Greeley where I worked as a civilian. They were so full of questions revolving around what is going on in my life now and my plans for the future. I've decided to catch you up on what is happening in my life up to this point. As for the future, well that is another chapter that has yet to be written. I want you to know that to read this is your option and I encourage you to delete this e-mail if it is not of interest, as I would hate to be accused of sending out junk mail. ☺

At the moment we are in the process of refitting our unit, repairing and replacing equipment as needed, and continuing with training. I'm going to get my first high altitude free-fall in 12 years next week! Yippee! In all reality, I have about another 45 days before I will know what lies ahead. In the meantime, I have been attempting to make the best of the situation.

I've now been home approximately one month. When we returned to Fort Carson it became apparent that with the number of troops mobilized for Iraq and currently stationed at Carson, we would be forced to stay in a hotel. Well, twist my arm! What a change from the past seven months…I'm sure I don't have to go into detail on this if you've been reading my previous e-mails.

We were given a week at Fort Carson to "decompress" after our 30-hour flight home. My wonderful parents drove up to meet me and deliver my truck, which had been in storage in Oklahoma. We were able to spend a few hours together for a couple of days, meeting around my schedule with the Army. One morning my parents met me at my hotel's restaurant for breakfast. Since I was going to Carson immediately after breakfast, I was wearing my desert camouflage uniform. A table of four middle-aged patrons had just finished their meal, and as they were leaving they stopped at our table. They addressed me and thanked me for my service. The ladies hugged me and the men shook my hand. I was humbled by this as I was sitting with my mother and father, and Dad is a veteran of World War II. To me, he and his generation are the heroes.

My parents stayed in Colorado for a few days before heading back to Oklahoma. I knew that I would be seeing them again soon.

During the past three weeks one of the things that has floored me is the number of people, complete strangers, who have approached me and thanked me for defending the country. Unbelievable! Sometimes restaurant owners have given me a complimentary meal; other times patrons have picked up the tab. I believe that some people were expressing their gratitude, while others who couldn't serve saw this as their way of contributing to the war effort. I'm sure that some of the people were passing along the thanks they received when they came home from their combat tours in the past, or maybe some never got thanked. Whatever the reason, it has been quite a poignant experience for me, something I did not expect.

Colorado was still experiencing winter snow storms, so in my mind, the countryside was not much different from Afghanistan, except, of course, the buildings, people, traffic, etc. After our decompression week, we were allowed to take a pass. I managed to make my way down to Duncan, Oklahoma, to see my parents and friends. The 11-hour drive to Oklahoma brought back a rush of memories. This is a drive I have made many times and it was interesting to see the changes that had occurred in the landscape along the route. Most interesting to me was how green the scenery became the further south I drove, and when I hit the Oklahoma border, the smell of freshly mowed grass came pouring into my vehicle through the ventilation system. It smelled so fresh, so alive, something that I had not sensed in many months. Another thing about Oklahoma that struck me was the number of birds singing. Again, this was something rarely heard in Afghanistan.

Upon my return, one of the first things on the agenda was to give an inspirational presentation on the war to my church in Duncan. Many of you reading this have now had the opportunity to see this presentation and, from what I hear, have enjoyed it. The First Christian Church of Duncan gave me a warm welcome home. There were many faces I recognized in the audience, along with many new faces who had come to meet the Captain Diggs they had come to know through my e-mails. This was the first time I had the opportunity to speak to anyone about my experiences in Afghanistan. I really wanted to get the message out about the good that we Americans are doing in this desolate country. I did get a bit emotional at times, especially when I was asked about the children who were accidentally killed in the training incident.

The congregation of the church had sent school supplies to our project school at Pol-e-charkhi, and I made sure they knew just how much those contributions, and the contributions sent by all of you, meant to the future of the Afghan children. I am so thankful that I was able to give this speech because I needed to get some things out of my system—and what better way to do this than to share with friends?

While in Duncan I also managed to get in some golf with my good friends, have dinner with new and old acquaintances, and have an interview with the local newspaper. The interview gave me a chance, once again, to reinforce the reality that Americans are the most generous people on the planet. Without their help those poor kids at Pol-e-charkhi would be in a very bad situation.

I really thought that my time in Duncan would allow me to unwind, but to my dismay I continued to wake up at 3:00 a.m. and lie in bed until I fell back to sleep a couple of hours later. To this day I am still having a hard time sleeping, and I can't even begin to figure out why. I guess there are just too many things on my mind. I am also still hacking up Afghan dust from deep down in my lungs. YUK!

I should also mention that while in Duncan I gave three presentations to the high school ROTC students. Not all of these kids are going to go on to a military career. However, I hope the ones who do will take a lesson with them, and the students who will go on to other endeavors will come to appreciate the things that perhaps they are taking for granted.

While in Oklahoma, I was invited by a teacher at Westfall Elementary (near Choctaw) to come and meet the children with whom I had been exchanging letters. These elementary students had read my e-mails in regard to the poor school conditions in Afghanistan and had sent over a large shipment of educational supplies. This was all of their own accord; I never asked for anything directly from them. They felt the need to give something to children they had never met on the other side of the world. Who says that the kids today are self-centered?

Dad came along with me on this presentation. Pulling into the school, we noticed the marquee at the entrance. It read, "Welcome Captain Diggs." Wow! We arrived a bit early and were met by three of the most polite children who introduced themselves and escorted us to the principal's office. The children at this school were well behaved with good manners. After introductions to the staff and a quick bite of breakfast, Dad and I were escorted to the gymnasium where I was to set up my computer and projector. Before we got to the gym, we were shown a large bulletin board that had several of the pictures I had e-mailed to the children, along with an American flag that at one time flew over our base in Afghanistan.

When the children entered the gym (grades kindergarten through sixth) I was floored. There were over 600 students and some of their parents; many of them had made banners and hand-held signs welcoming me. This was nothing I expected. After a few school announcements, I was introduced and gave my presentation. When it came time for questions and answers, these children wasted no time in coming up with intelligent questions that I would have imagined beyond their scope of reason. I was told over and over again by these kids that I was their hero. This was a very impressive and very touching experience for me, without a doubt.

My father and I had a conversation about the day's events during the drive home. Although I was astonished that I was regarded as a hero, Dad gave me a good lesson:

Don't confuse fame with heroism; they are two different things. The common bond that most heroes have is the willingness to make some sort of sacrifice for others—possibly life, limb, comfort, cash, time, or convenience; the list goes on and on. I am convinced that anyone can be a hero. It is a choice that you make, and it comes from the heart. There are so many different avenues to heroism, not necessarily on the battlefield.

A couple of things caught my attention when I was at my parents' home in Duncan. They had saved back issues of several major magazines. Thumbing through these publications and reading the letters to the editors and the "end of the world" articles, it became apparent to me that many people do not comprehend what is really happening in the war. I hope that my presentations can get the word out that we Americans are doing great things on a global scale, and when there is trouble in the world, most nations turn their eyes to us for help.

Something else that really ticks me off is hearing people say, "I support the troops, but not the war." To hell with that; you can't have your cake and eat it, too. I guarantee you that none of the soldiers believe that statement has any validity.

One other thing I want to point out in regard to the press is that they tend to focus on the Hollywood celebrities who are against the war. Who in the world are the Dixie Chicks, and where do they get off berating my president? I saw very little mention of the stars who supported the troops and came over to entertain us. Karri Turner of "JAG" fame and Darryl Worley, a country/western singer, both came to our location and continue to see the troops to this day. Where was that mentioned? How about Robin Williams, Bruce Willis, Jay Leno, David Letterman, and others? They all came, but where would you see that in print? Hollywood is not as liberal as one would think, but try and get that story out to the public.

Moving on.

My next stop for a presentation was two weeks ago at Northeast Elementary School in Parker, Colorado. They had made a very generous donation of school supplies and clothing. On the exterior of the school was a large handmade sign welcoming me with the familiar moniker "Captain Diggs." When I was escorted into the classroom, you should have seen these kids' faces light up! We had a short time to get acquainted before I gave my presentation, and I finally got to meet Hally, who was my pen pal from this school. There were to a total of three classes combined for the presentation with all of the children very enthusiastic for the show. Once again, the children asked such intelligent questions. Their parents and teachers can be proud of what they have accomplished. These children, of their own accord, gave the gift of education to the impoverished children halfway across the world.

I have been appointed as my unit's public affairs officer and am responsible for coordinating interviews and appearances. We have had several newspapers come and interview the troops, and all have gone extremely well. There seems to be a great deal of interest in the "citizen soldiers" and our contribution to the war effort. This war was the first time our unit has been activated for combat operations.

The Holocaust and eventual liberation from the concentration camps is celebrated by the Jewish community with Holocaust Remembrance Week every April 29th. The 157th Infantry Regiment from Colorado played a major roll in freeing the prisoners at Dachua, the first camp liberated. As part of the celebration, two other officers and I were invited to Denver take part in the commemoration of the anniversary. The tie-in was liberators of the past and present. I met the heroes from the 157th and some of the prisoners they had freed. Wow! One of the prisoners had survived six years in three different concentration camps and then went on to join the American army in the Korean War! After that war he was awarded his citizenship. What an impressive gathering of American patriots and heroes!

What amazed me about the ceremony was the number of Holocaust survivors and soldiers who were thanking us for fighting our war. In my mind, it was the other way around, and I let them know that was my belief. The ceremony was very solemn and yet inspiring. The photos of the concentration camps and the eventual liberation spoke volumes. How could such horrid events take place? And yet, we are dealing with the same mentality today in the Taliban, Hussein, al Qaeda, and other countries yet to be determined. Considering the history of dictators, how can the French and Germans turn their backs on the obvious? I wouldn't expect anything other than that from the Russians.

A few days ago 15 of us were invited to attend the Denver Chamber of Commerce's luncheon. General Meyers, Chairman of the Joint Chiefs of Staff, was the guest speaker. We were honored to accept the invitation for the meeting at the Brown Palace, which is not only one of Denver's most posh hotels, but one of the oldest. It was built by "The Unsinkable Molly Brown." At this event we were once again treated like royalty, and the general's speech was impressive. I am thoroughly convinced that President Bush has surrounded himself with a very capable and intelligent staff, to his credit. The basis of Meyers's speech was that wars are being won by the quality of training, equipment, and soldiers. He further stated that we are a long way from the end of the global war on terrorism. He was well received and took time after the luncheon to personally thank us for our contribution. He is a remarkable man indeed.

Yesterday I made my way up to Greeley to give a presentation to my bank and also to a high school and grade school. At the bank were some familiar faces and some new ones, too. Due to the short notice I gave, not all who wished to come could make it, but yet, those who did made my day. It was genuinely good to see my friends and have a chance to share my experience with them. It seemed that their concern was more about when I would return to the bank as an employee, and I wish I could have given them an answer.

At the high school, I gave two presentations to several classes in the auditorium. I was amazed that I was able to hold the attention of the number of teenagers present. This fact says a lot for their teachers and the interest level in world events. Several of the students came up afterward and thanked me for coming in. Three wanted to join the military, much to the joy of the recruiter who accompanied me. Now *there* is a sharp businessman!

After the high school presentations, I was guided over to Meeker Elementary just a few blocks away. I had been kept in the dark regarding the events at this school. I assumed that I would be giving my presentation as usual, but things were much different, to my surprise. First, let me preface this with the fact that these third and fourth graders had been diligent in writing. Two in particular, De and Jackson, had become regular pen pals.

This class had also sent gifts to the students in Afghanistan and piles of letters to me. I was escorted to the classroom. To my astonishment, it was decorated with red, white, and blue streamers. The children were all standing in their chairs greeting me! Beyond this were a number of parents, including the parents of Caroline Street, the teacher. Her parents had also been corresponding with me and had at one time sent several boxes of cookies.

The children all came up and introduced themselves to me, and during a flurry of photographs, they presented me with a gift of a beaded American flag that they all had participated in constructing. Next came the reading of letters that were written before I came home, but not sent due to time constraints. The authors stood in their chairs and read aloud their compositions. I want to share one of those with you. The young man who wrote it is named Jackson.

Dear Captain Diggs,

Hey! This is Jackson. I just wanted to say thanks for the awesome hats. With my hat, I wore it for the whole day I got it. It now is with all my other special stuff. In all of my life, these three words have always remained a mystery in meaning, God Bless America, until now.

I now know that there are thousands of brave souls who go to join the army to defend our nation (including yourself). This simple yet meaningful phrase means "God is with us." It means we don't commit suicide for the purpose of killing others. This means we are a free country, one that does not need to be forced to join the army, but one that goes at our free will to defend our nation.

Gold Bless America; this phrase will remain in my life forever.

I also wanted to say thanks for everything. We're more proud of you than you can imagine.

> *Sincerely,*
> *Jackson*

When the letter reading was finished, I gave my presentation and answered questions. We got hung up on the subject of ringworms for a few minutes after viewing the photo of a poor little boy at the medical mission. After admitting my ignorance on the subject of ringworms, we moved on to the war once again and finished the presentation.

Lunch was served in the school cafeteria and we were served French fries (excuse me, Freedom fries), chicken sandwiches and salad, which we ate in the classroom. There were more photos taken with all the children and parents. Finally it was time to depart. The children gave me heartfelt hugs and I was off, a richer man for the experience.

As in life, there never seems to be enough time—time being our most precious commodity. There is a school in Sterling, Colorado, that I would like to visit and meet the children who sent supplies to Afghanistan; but alas, I won't be able to make my way there before the school year is over. There are so many people I'd love to meet in person and thank for their efforts and support. I could spend weeks traveling and probably still not have enough time to accomplish this task. I hope all understand the time constraints.

THANK YOU FOR ALL THE SUPPORT!

Sincerely,
Diggs

CHAPTER 25 • HOME AT LAST!

CHAPTER 26
LAST THOUGHTS

Somewhere in the past decade or so, we Americans lost sight of what it takes to be a hero. Suddenly there was September 11, 2001, and there has been a great emphasis placed on heroism and a rediscovering of what the true meaning is. In fact, I have used the term hero many times in my letters. Our definition of heroes has gone through a great rejuvenation and is worth revisiting. No longer should there be the misconception that fame makes one a hero. Athletes are just that, athletes. Entertainers are just that, entertainers. Very few, if any at all, have made the sacrifices we should associate with heroes. The Webster's definition of hero is:

> An individual of distinguished valor or enterprise in danger, or fortitude in suffering; a prominent or central personage in any remarkable action or event; hence, a great or illustrious person.

Foremost in my mind, the first heroes of 9/11 are the firefighters, police, and other emergency personnel who charged up the World Trade Towers, knowing full well that they were risking life and limb to save those trapped on the upper floors. Many of these men had taken magic markers and scrawled their social security numbers on their arms and legs in case the buildings collapsed, crushing them beyond recognition. Even after the first tower buckled, these brave men still attempted to rescue the innocents of Tower Two, only to make the ultimate sacrifice. How many countless lives were saved by their sacrifices? All gave some; some gave all.

The list of heroes continues with those who have served in the Armed Forces, past and present, in the global war on terror. Many have made the ultimate sacrifice to protect all Americans and the liberties we cherish. There was little concern for self, but concern for the common cause—freedom.

I have to tell you that I served with a battalion full of heroes. My unit was composed of "citizen soldiers" who left their homes, families, and occupations to fight this just and noble war. Some got divorced while we were away, some took massive pay cuts, some missed seeing the birth of their children; all gave something. In particular, two soldiers I mentioned in my letters home are my heroes, Doc Enz and Chaplain Andy.

Doc Enz, while not a "warrior hero," took time and made the effort to correct the vision of so many children. He gave his time and technical expertise to make a difference in the lives of kids who never would have received help otherwise. He gave them the gift of sight.

Chaplain Andy organized and conducted both teaching and food contributions for the school children and orphans. He did this without expecting a thank you and with no concern for his personal safety. He did it out of the goodness of his heart; he made a difference.

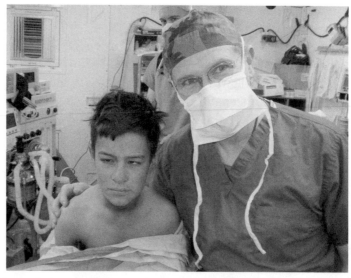

Doc Enzenhauer prepares to correct this child's crossed eyes. His efforts were well above the call of duty and had a significant impact on the lives of the children he operated on.

Keep in mind that many of you reading this are possibly heroes and don't realize it. The grade school children who sent school donations are heroes. We should be proud of this generation. It does not necessarily take a war to make one a hero, but it does take a choice—and that choice is yours. You must be willing to give and to sacrifice for others. Honor the heroes, and live your life the way they would have wanted you to.

Something that has made me the proudest is to have the American flag sewn on the right sleeve of my uniform. I am proud to serve my country, and it has been my honor to defend you and your way of life. I wouldn't have exchanged this experience for anything in the world. I cannot express to you how taken aback I have been over the past few weeks with the outpouring of gratitude from friends and strangers alike.

Most important of all is that I want you to understand that the e-mails of the past 12 months have not been about me, they have been about you. The whole shared experience has shown that life as we know it revolves around human compassion—the compassion of students, parents, teachers, strangers, and friends. We Americans excel at this.

It is also about the American spirit, the willingness to seek out and help those in need. It is selfless sacrifice on the part of a country that comes as liberators, not conquerors. No other country in history has done so much to help others in need, and I doubt if any will. We rarely hear a thank you from the world for what we have done for them. But you know what, we don't give expecting a thank you; we give because we are Americans.

We Americans are a people who prize freedom above all else. We understand that freedom is a right granted by God to every being on our planet, and we understand there is a God. It is our desire to spread freedom around the world so that people can be lifted from oppression and realize their God-given rights. As the Special Forces motto states, "Liberate the oppressed." Americans can overcome any adversity with or without our allies and *so called allies*. Our spirit, our belief in a higher being, has shaped us as a nation. Our generations of the past and the present are making sacrifices, as will our future generations. Sometimes these sacrifices are for us; sometimes they are for a faceless nation on the other side of the world. We will continue to be the world leader, and this is our Manifest Destiny.

In closing, I want to thank all of you for your support in this great endeavor. My life has changed dramatically, and I am positive that yours have also. Your support, prayers, generous gifts to the children of Afghanistan, comfort items you sent me, letters, and e-mails were appreciated well beyond your comprehension. You have touched the lives of people on the other side of the world and mine also. I will never forget it.

With all respect and gratitude, thank you.
Captain Diggs
United States Army Special Forces

Photo Credits:
B. Diggs Brown
Shannon Davidson
Chaplain Andy Meverden
Dean Vavra

Poetic Contributions:
Robert Burns
Rudyard Kipling
Angus Steele
William Shakespeare

About the Author

Diggs Brown is a professional speaker, successful businessman, Green Beret officer, author, and photographer.

Beyond his ability to turn around marginal businesses, creating a positive and profitable environment, Diggs has the unique skill to inspire people to strive to better themselves and others. He brings teams together and leads them, or trains their leaders, to achieve goals once thought unattainable.

Diggs has been a featured guest on both television and radio sharing his knowledge of teamwork and inspiration. He has been a constant in the volatile world of corporate change, leading and mentoring others to success. Diggs has an incredible amount of experience and motivation to share with others seeking to better themselves and achieve success.

To this day, he continues to serve in the Colorado Army National Guard. In his civilian life, beyond professional speaking, he enjoys golf, the Harley Davidson he bought while in Afghanistan, hiking the Rocky Mountains, and service in his church.

Diggs is available to give motivational and inspirational presentations to your organization. He can be reached on his website www.diggs.us. Additional copies of *Your Neighbor Went to War* may be purchased on this site. Contact us for bulk orders.

GLOSSARY

Al Jazeera – a biased Arab news network

al Qaeda – Muslim terrorist organization headed by Osama bin Laden

Bagram – major city north of Kabul, Afghanistan. A key U.S. Air Force base is located there.

Bedouin – Arab nomads

concertina – coiled barbed wire placed on top of walls and fences for security

Dari – one of the two major languages used in Afghanistan

DFAC – Dining Facility; replacing the former term of "mess hall"

firebase – a base of operation in a remote location

haggis – a mix of oatmeal, sausage, and blood that is cooked inside a sheep's stomach

Hajiks – tribe indigenous to southwest Asia

Hizb-i-Islami – a radical Muslim group known for its extreme views and ruthless dealings with non-followers

hooch – military slang for "living quarters"

hot load – when an aircraft continues to run its engines while loading or unloading passengers or equipment

ISAF – International Security Assistance Force, a military coalition comprised of 24 allied nations assisting in operations in Afghanistan

Jalalabad Road – the main highway through Kabul leading to Jalalabad

KMTC – Kabul Military Training Center

lorries – British term for trucks

madrasas – a building or group of buildings used for teaching Islamic theology and religious law, typically including a mosque

MEDCAPs – Medical Civil Assistance Program or Medical Capabilities Mission

MREs – "meals ready to eat" prepackaged for use by U.S. military

Mujahedeen – Muslim guerrilla warriors engaged in jihad

Northern Alliance – Afghan tribesmen aligned against the Taliban

Operation Anaconda – large U.S. military operation in eastern Afghanistan

Pashtuns – tribe indigenous to southwest Asia

PETA – People for the Ethical Treatment of Animals

Pol-e-charkhi – town on the outskirts of eastern Kabul

PX – Post Exchange—a store located on a military base

SF – Special Forces

strack – strictly by the rules and regulations

Tajiks – tribe indigenous to southwest Asia

Taliban – fundamentalist Muslim government established in Afghanistan in 1989

Tora Bora – mountainous region of eastern Afghanistan

Uaz – Russian jeeps

wadis – valleys, gullies, or streambeds in northern Africa and southwest Asia that remain dry except during the rainy season

AFGHANISTAN QUICK FACTS

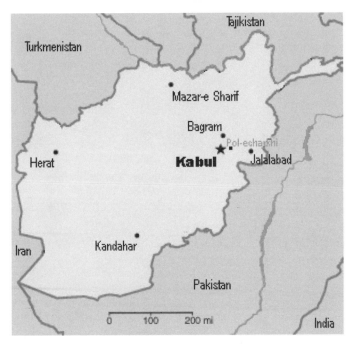

Area:	647,500 square miles, slightly smaller than Texas
Border Countries:	China, Iran, Pakistan, Tajikistan, Turkmenistan, Uzbekistan
Terrain:	Rugged mountain with plains in the north and southwest
Elevation:	Low – 846 feet above sea level High – 24,557 feet above sea level
Population:	29,001,433
Life Expectancy:	42.5 years
Ethic Groups:	Pashtun 42%, Tajik 27%, Hazara 9%, Uzbeck 9%, Aimak 4%, Turkmen 3%, Baloch 2%, other 4%
Religion:	Sunni Muslim 80%, Shi's Muslim 19%, other 1%
Languages:	Pashtu (official language) 35%, Dari 50%, Turkic 11%, 30 minor languages 4%